About the Author

James Van Praagh is arguably the most famous and successful spiritual medium of our time, world-renowned for his extraordinary ability to communicate with the spirits of men, women, children and animals who have died. His lectures, demonstrations and spiritual tours have drawn many thousands of people round the world. He has been a featured guest on *The Oprah Winfrey Show*, *Larry King Live* and countless other television and radio shows, as well as being interviewed in *The New York Times* and elsewhere. He lives in the Los Angeles area.

Looking

*How to Use Your Psychic Talent
to Get What You Want Out of Life*

Beyond

James Van Praagh

RIDER

LONDON • SYDNEY • AUCKLAND • JOHANNESBURG

9 10 8

Published in 2003 by Rider, an imprint of Ebury Publishing
First published in the USA by Fireside, an imprint of Simon & Schuster Inc., in
2003

Ebury Publishing is a Random House Group company

The Random House Group Limited Reg. No. 954009

Addresses for companies within the Random House Group can be found at
www.rbooks.co.uk

A CIP catalogue record for this book is available from the British Library

The Random House Group Limited supports The Forest Stewardship
Council (FSC), the leading international forest certification organisation. All our
titles that are printed on Greenpeace approved FSC certified paper carry the FSC
logo. Our paper procurement policy can be found at
www.rbooks.co.uk/environment

Designed by Ruth Lee

Printed and bound in Great Britain by
CPI Antony Rowe, Chippenham, Wiltshire

ISBN 9781844132171

Copies are available at special rates for bulk orders. Contact the sales
development team on 020 7840 8487 or visit www.booksforpromotions.co.uk
for more information.

To buy books by your favourite authors and register for offers, visit
www.rbooks.co.uk

To Brian,
for always being my sunshine in all kinds of weather.

Acknowledgments

Linda Carwin Tomchin—Thank you for yet another reincarnation! You give my words meaning and my message wings to fly. You are truly one of heaven's finest.

Kelly Dennis—I have never been the same since meeting you! Your gifts of laughter, song, and dance always uplift my soul. Thank you for helping me remember how to be a kid again!

Kelley Kreinbrink—You are a blessing in my life. Thank you for keeping me organized and always giving me life support!

Phyllis Heller—I appreciate you always being there talking twice as fast as any other New Yorker I have ever met! Thank you for your dedication, friendship, and trust in taking this journey together.

Contents

Let Me Introduce Myself

My name is James, and I am a psychic and a medium. As a medium, I am able to contact the dead and communicate their messages to the living. I have been doing this for the past twenty years.

You may have seen me on television, doing readings for people. When I read for people, I tune in to their energy to feel around them a spirit who wants to tell them something. I have done thousands of individual readings for people all over the world. After a while, I started to do these readings in front of large audiences. I call these large-group gatherings demonstrations.

Over the years, many people have come to me with stories filled with tragedy and love, seeking guidance, healing, and peace with loved ones who have passed on. I hope that I have been able to put their minds and hearts at ease.

The gift I have is not extraordinary, though many have said so. I believe that everyone has psychic awareness, but few have the patience, understanding, or perhaps the desire to develop it the way that I have. I did not fully utilize my psychic abilities until I became an adult, but I was very aware of them as a child. A lot of patience and years of practice went into the work I do today.

The truth is that everything you want to know is already inside you. That is why I wrote this book: I want you to recognize that you are a spiritual being who is a part of a large cosmic family of spiritual beings. As you learn that there is more to you than meets the eye, you will find that you have the power, strength, and talent to fulfill your own individual earthly destiny. May your journey be filled with love.

Spirits in a Material World

Look Inside, and All Will Be Revealed

I See Dead People

When I was a young boy, I used to see ghosts all the time, like the kid in *The Sixth Sense*. It was like one giant ghost party around me. I used to see people standing in my room just as I was going to sleep. Sometimes, they would pop up when I got into trouble. It wasn't scary or creepy like in the movie, though. Actually, it was quite the opposite. My ghosts had kind faces. They were gentle, not spooky. Mostly, they were family members who had died, like my grandfather or aunt. They just wanted me to know that they were watching over me like guardian angels.

To me, these ghosts appeared as solid forms with heads and bodies just like everyone else I knew. The only difference between the living and the dead was the beautiful glowing light that surrounded the ghosts. And when the ghosts spoke to me, it was a mind-to-mind communication—no one ever moved their lips.

Frankly, I thought my ability to see ghosts was pretty cool. I was

quite innocent, though, and thought everyone else could see ghosts, too. It wasn't until I was hanging out with a few friends and told them about my ghostly visions that I found out I was very different. But while my friends thought I was ready for the loony bin, I didn't think of myself as a freak. I knew in my heart that what my friends were saying about me was not true. They couldn't see ghosts, but I knew what I saw, and I knew it was real.

I didn't have a clue about how life really worked until I understood why ghosts appeared to me. It was a pretty simple, yet far-out, idea. It certainly didn't fit the picture of life that I was being taught. Time after time, spirits impress upon me the idea that all of us, dead or alive, are purely spiritual in nature. We are not human beings, but spirit beings in human bodies.

So, in this book, I want to share my thoughts about how life really works, what I have learned from all the spirit beings who have contacted me. If we all knew who we really are, we might have a better understanding of ourselves and others.

Who Do You Think You Are?

How many times have you looked at the stars and wondered what lies beyond them? Could there be other life in far-off galaxies? Could there be alien life forms right here on our planet? Of course there are. Wasn't that what they were trying to tell us in the movie *Men in Black*?

But have you ever wondered who *you* are and what *you* are doing here on this planet?

My take on this whole question goes like this: You and I are students in one giant classroom. Like those "men in black," you and I are here to uncover the truth underneath these alien bodies we are wearing. It's simple for me to say, but finding out who we are is something people have been trying to figure out for a long time.

Just think about a time when you went along with a friend's idea just because you thought you wanted to be part of the crowd or to look cool to the others. Even though inside you felt that it really wasn't what you wanted to do, you did it anyway. I've been there, too.

The first thing I learned from spirits was to pay attention to feelings. Our emotions and intuition, those voices inside, have something to tell us. Too often, especially as we get older, we put such feelings aside and rely more on what we see and hear, not to mention the influence of others on us. In this book, I am going to stress the importance of feelings: paying attention to your feelings is one of the best ways to help you learn who you are and what's right for you.

Feel Everything You Can

It takes a lot of courage and honesty to follow your own feelings about things. Think of feelings as the road map, and your life as the journey. Feelings can guide you to all the right roads, on-ramps, and off-ramps, as well as the rest stops in between.

Everyone feels differently, so no one can tell you what you are really feeling or how to feel it. Still, identifying your feelings and how they are affecting your behavior may be difficult at first. Sometimes, it just seems easier to go along with the popular consensus. I don't know many people who want to rock the boat or stand out in a crowd. However, if you pay attention to your feelings, especially when you don't want to follow the crowd, you will begin to understand what makes you uniquely you.

> ## Your feelings are a clue to what's going on inside you.

Let's Hit the Road

So now, with that being said, if you would like to begin the journey to uncover the real you, step right up and grab some supplies. Let's find the spirit being that is lurking around in your body.

SOUL SUPPLIES

- **Courage to question the world as you see it**
- **Feelings to know who you are**
- **Honesty to stay true to your feelings**

Looking Beyond

- ⟡ **Imagination to create whatever you want**
- ⟡ **Questions about what you allow into your mind and heart**
- ⟡ **Faith to believe in your feelings and thoughts when no one else does**

Last, but not least, be ready for some reality checks to help you along the way. How are you going to know what reality you want if you don't know there are many to choose from?

Now, step up to the starting line.

The *real you* journey starts here.

Signpost #1: The world is not as it seems.

Life Is Only a Game

The Matrix is a movie that made us think differently about our world. For those of you who haven't seen it, the movie is about people who are going about their everyday lives, until one day they realize that life is just a projection of a computer program called the Matrix. Things seem real, feel real, but in fact every human being is controlled by the program. People are kept docile and compliant, sort of like mindless slaves who cannot think for themselves. Sound familiar?

However, Keanu Reeves's character is quite smart and soon learns

how to maneuver through the computer game. One of the ways he does is by not believing everything he sees. Because he can manipulate the program better than most, the others think that he's "the one." The movie plot thickens as one of the rebels turns traitor and decides to join forces with the Matrix. This leads the others to an all-out tug-of-war against the Matrix in order to free the human species from enslavement and deception.

The movie definitely struck a chord in everyone who saw it. Most of us want to break out of the "reality" of our lives and transcend our limitations. If life is a game like the Matrix, then we all want to know the truth, so we can play it better. We want to be aware of the bullets and bullies so that we can get out of their way. Everybody wants to tap into extraordinary possibilities and perhaps even be "the one." So how do we do it? The first step is to start seeing the world differently.

Cell Phones, Microphones, and All Those Crazy Electromagnetic Waves

The energy waves that make our cell phones, TVs, and microwave ovens work are invisible to the naked eye, even as they move through the universe all the time. A hundred years ago, we didn't know much about this energy, and didn't even dream of these devices, but we use these things every day without giving them a second thought. The same type of energy waves that connect us instantaneously today existed back then, too. It took someone to see the world differently in order to discover this energy and put it to use.

While we live on earth we occupy physical bodies. It's the way we get around on earth. Our bodies keep us from crashing into one another. Think of your body as your home, and you are the spirit being living inside it. Your body is merely ENERGY made of molecules—atoms, electrons, protons, subatomic particles—that kind of stuff you tend to forget after the chemistry exam, but the same kind of stuff that makes your cell phone work.

In fact, the whole universe is an energy field. This energy moves at various rates of speed. In the physical world of matter, where we reside, these molecules move very, very slowly. That's why our bodies and the rest of the physical world appear solid.

In the higher spiritual dimensions, however, the energy moves very quickly, and physical bodies are not necessary because they could not contain the faster-moving energy. That's why spirit beings are invisible to us; they flash by us faster than our physical eyes can actually see.

This energy is a powerful force—it is what you and I are made of and where we come from. THIS ENERGY IS THE REAL YOU. That means we are not just material girls . . . or guys. We are spirits living in a material world.

So, the REAL YOU is actually camouflaged by your body. The real you is actually a beam of light, pure energy, vibrating in different colors. You can't see this beam of light because your body is so dense. Some people, like me, can see it. I see colors around people all the time. I see their *auras*.

Sometimes you can see this beam of light, too, when you look into someone's eyes. You see their soul's light shining out. That's what attracts us to one another.

Your eyes are the windows of your soul.

Do You Measure Yourself by Your Jeans?

Most of the time, we think of ourselves as limited human beings because all we see are our bodies. And let's face it: our bodies can do only so much. The mistake is that we identify ourselves AS our bodies. We think our bodies are the whole enchilada. Don't get me wrong—bodies

Real style comes from inside.

are important, because they transport us all around the planet. They want to keep on ticking so the real you inside can enjoy life.

Still, we do spend a lot of our time and energy worrying about what we look like. It doesn't take much for bad hair and pimples to spoil a perfectly good day. I know it's no fun to break out when you're about to go on a special date, but believe me, no one is paying attention to your zits when he or she is looking into those soul-filled eyes of yours.

By focusing on the body, we spend much too much time judging ourselves and others by outward appearances. Why waste time critiquing others based on whether or not they're wearing the latest Tommy Hilfiger jeans or Reebok Iverson basketball shoes? It's easy to be impressed by a nice-looking package, but it's the gift inside that counts. The real reason we want to look good is to feel loved and accepted for who we really are.

Spirits Living in a Material World

If everyone is a spirit being, what about the people you don't like? They're spirit beings, too—everyone is energy, and this energy is vibrating all the time. It travels from one person to another. Just because we can't see it doesn't mean it's not there.

Some people have a lot of anxiety, fear, and hatred; some are light and free and full of fun.

James Van Praagh

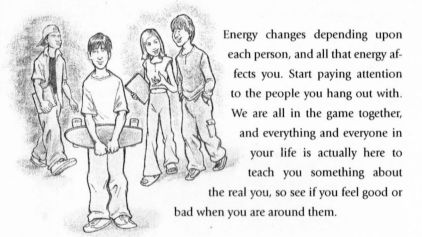

Energy changes depending upon each person, and all that energy affects you. Start paying attention to the people you hang out with. We are all in the game together, and everything and everyone in your life is actually here to teach you something about the real you, so see if you feel good or bad when you are around them.

What's the Point?

We all have been tricked into believing that we are limited beings— limited by our own minds and what we think is important on the material level, things like clothes, grades, dating, looks, popularity, and so forth. Just remember that you are really not what you appear to be. You are an excellent, unlimited light being. That is the power of your spiritual self. The more you realize that you are a spiritual being in human form, the more you become aware of your energy force, and the more you are prepared to deal with life on a human level. You have the ability to change any condition in your life. What an energizing and empowering realization!

When you feel empowered, you actually feel like jumping up and dancing. You have energy; you feel in control of your life. You become a powerful force. Things that once seemed overwhelming—getting good grades, talking to your parents, getting a date with someone you think is terrific—are not so hard.

When I was a teen, I didn't have much direction in my life. I wish someone had given me a clue as to how life really worked. If I had known I was really a spirit being in human form, I might have had more confidence in myself. That's what I hope you get from this book—a sense that you are a great person, filled with incredible abilities and the power to accomplish what you want. You can do this, no matter what other people may want you to do or be. Yes, there are pitfalls and problems. Don't let these things overcome you. Use this guide to foster an *I can do it!* attitude in the exciting game we call life.

SPIRIT SAYS . . .

You are a spirit being in a material world.
Your energy is a powerful force.
It's hard to be who you are when you do what
someone else wants.
Live from the inside out, not the outside in.
Let your feelings guide your way.

Write something about how you feel right now or about your life in general.

_____

_____

_____

_____

_____

Here We Go Again!

The Wheel of Life Goes Round and Round

The School of Hard Knocks

Okay, now that you get the idea about who you are, the next question: Why are you here?

Simply put, you planned this life in advance before coming to earth. Like I said, earth is a classroom, and we are students learning as much as we can so we can perfect ourselves. Think of yourself as a diamond in the rough. How you handle your experiences, and what you learn from them, is how you are cut and polished. Each situation that is resolved with love reveals another beautiful facet of yourself. When you have gone through the total range of experiences that life has to offer with love and compassion, you have reached perfection. You return home to the heart of God, and live forever in a world that is too beautiful for our minds to grasp.

Why is all this necessary? Why can't we just have fun hanging out and skip all the growing and learning stuff?

Well, I think of it this way. Have you ever had such an incredible dream that when you woke up, you felt happy? Maybe you dreamed of being at a Britney Spears concert and were asked on stage. There you were singing along with the pop star, and to your amazement, you had this incredible voice. You felt on top of the world. The dream seemed so real because the good feelings were still with you when you woke up . . . then you realized it was only a dream, and it was just another ordinary day. You wanted so much to go back to being in the dream, having a good time, and feeling great.

That's the feeling you get as you grow more spiritually. It seems that the more we learn and grow on this earth, the better we feel about our ordinary lives. One day when we graduate from this earth, we go back to that great dream place and never have to leave it again.

Here is another way of looking at it. Think of your relationship with your best friend. The more the two of you help each other learn about things going on, and what to do and what not to do, the more you nurture your relationship. You get on the phone with each other and talk for hours—your parents wonder what you two could possibly talk about for so long. But you are learning about your own tastes and habits as well as your friend's. Your friendship grows with each passing day, and you and your friend get to share a lot of experiences together and in the process create a lot of great memories.

These types of earthly experiences feed our souls. The more we learn about life, our friends, our habits, the more we go through ups and downs with one another, the more beautifully our souls develop. Our souls want these earthly experiences because as we learn about keeping a friendship, or how to solve a problem, or what makes us happy, we progress as spiritual beings.

What Is Your Soul?

Your soul is the essence and sum total of who you are from the beginning of time. Every thought, word, action, feeling, and millisecond of your lifetimes on earth and in the spirit worlds are part of your soul's memory. This comes in handy, because the things you learn in one lifetime stay with you in the next, and you don't have to take that particular class over again. It's a "been there, done that" kind of thing.

I believe we live over and over again, not in the same body, but in different bodies and in different places. Through my own spiritual teachers who work with me, I have learned that when we decide to return to earth and master new opportunities for growth, we map out a plan for the earthly existence while still in the spiritual realms. During this process, we decide on the circumstances and events we want to encounter. We choose our sex, our nationality, our race, our country, everything that will support our plan for a new life on earth—you get the idea. We do this so we can experience every possible lifestyle imaginable, to help work through our soul lessons—to learn how to relate to others, transform a situation for the better, or be more tolerant. For instance, if you were born in a country like India, South Africa, or China, you might have to learn to overcome hardship or to value life, and before assuming your earthly body, you picked that place for optimum growth.

Living over and over again is called reincarnation, and many millions of people all over the world believe in it—that they return to earth after each death and experience a new life as part of a continuous journey. Reincarnation is a pretty cool idea because it means we experience a variety of cultures and lives.

So, the next time you wonder how someone may know so much

about something, like that ten-year-old science whiz, the child prodigy who can play the piano like a pro at the age of six, or someone who is good in any sport he plays, you may begin to understand that these talents and abilities are a continuation of talents and abilities cultivated in other lifetimes. The same is true for you and your talents and abilities. Isn't it nice to know we don't have to start from scratch every time we come to earth?

Signpost #2: Your soul has a memory.

Haven't I Seen You Somewhere Before?

I am sure you have heard the term *déjà vu*. It's French, and literally it means "already seen." We use it to describe being in a situation that feels very familiar, as if you've been there before—and experienced it exactly the same way—but you know you haven't. Or, you meet someone new, and *boom!*, you feel an instant connection. In a déjà vu moment, you have tuned in to the awesome power of the soul and have been given a hint of a previous existence.

I remember the time I was driving through New Orleans with a bunch of friends. We stopped for dinner, and then suddenly I began to walk away from everyone as if in a trance.

"Where are you headed?" one friend asked.

"I don't know," I said. "But I have to see something around the corner."

My friends quickly followed behind.

"I am pretty sure there is a white church with two steeples around here," I continued.

Sure enough, when I reached the end of the block and turned the

I don't mind another body,
but can the clothes fit better this time?

corner, there was a white church with two steeples. The moment I saw it, I felt I had been in that church before.

I've experienced many such déjà vu hits in my life. On one of my spiritual odysseys in past-life regression through hypnosis, for example, I saw myself as sort of an Attila the Hun. There I was on some battlefield with my soldiers ready for me to give them the order to charge into battle. I was responsible for ordering thousands of soldiers to kill thousands of other soldiers. That vision gave me an insight into this life and why I am here: I see this life as

REALITY CHECK

Let's take a look at what I mean by *lifetimes*. Imagine a long rope, with maybe fifty knots in it spaced out every inch or so. Think of that rope as your soul, and each knot represents a lifetime. There is no break in the rope. It is one continuous line. That is what I mean by the soul being the totality of everything you are.

payback time. Instead of killing people, I now have a chance to heal them.

Soul Lessons

When we are born, everything we need to fulfill our souls' plan in this lifetime is buried deep within our souls. All those lifetimes of experience are piled up inside you, sort of like the stuff piled inside your locker. So, all the answers to all your problems are already within you, because your soul has accumulated a lot of wisdom.

"Not me!" you say. Yes, *even you.* Everyone comes equipped with all the necessary abilities, talents, and strategies to live life. Think of yourself as a tool chest. Inside you are all the tools necessary to complete any task you are faced with. For example, you have a quick mind: this comes in handy when you're figuring out math problems. Or, you have a gift of empathy and can tell if someone is having a hard time: your caring helps her get through a problem. Or, you are very active and like to try new adventures: it's no wonder you tend to excel in rock climbing and river rafting.

It is up to each of us to decide how quickly or slowly we want to learn, grow, and develop. The ups and downs of our lives are tests, or soul lessons, to see if we can uncover spiritual solutions to our problems. Your problems are really opportunities to learn and grow. Sometimes, you face similar problems from one life to the next—perhaps in this life you can figure out a better solution than you did in the last.

A friend of mine used to be totally uncoordinated. He would bump into people, knock things over, and break things without meaning to. He felt guilty about breaking things, and his father used to call him clumsy, which totally embarrassed him. I felt that his awkwardness was carried over from another lifetime, and suggested that he take a tai chi class. Eventually, my friend became more graceful and more self-assured.

Everyone is here to learn something. That's why everyone does things differently. You are here to learn something and your friend is here to learn something else. Learning never stops. This is where the idea of karma comes in.

Your Karma Hit My Dogma!

What goes around comes around. That's an easy way of explaining the term *karma*. Karma, in essence, equals action. There can be "good karma" and "bad karma." It's easy to remember: Whatever you give out, you will get back! For every *action* (cause) there is a *result* (effect).

Since we live many lifetimes, the karmic cycles of cause and effect can span lifetimes. In other words, the results of your actions in this life may not be settled in this life or even your next one; likewise, you may be settling in this life karmic issues from previous lives. But whether it's in this life or another, you get to balance your actions—your karma—at some point in the time/space paradigm of the material world.

For clarification purposes, I am not referring to the karma of the Hindu religion that has to do with social classes of the caste system, or coming back to a life in nonhuman form, i.e., as a bug or an animal.

People usually think of karma as something negative. It is not. It is about balance and neutrality. Think of karma as something like a bank account. Sometimes we add to the account and sometimes we subtract. At the end of the month, we have to reconcile our account to make sure our finances are in balance.

Her head was so big she could barely get through the door.

My Ego Thinks You're Hot

The biggest cause of negative karma is our egos. You know what I mean. Most of the time, we do things because we want to fit in or feel good or make an impression. That's our ego talking. Sometimes we do something for all the wrong reasons, just to be accepted.

Take Amy. She was an honor student, popular with her friends, and always had a date. At a party, Amy met Chad, who seemed to be nice and interested in her. At the time, she didn't know that he was going out with Cathy. Amy and Chad hit it off, and Amy became infatuated with him. Her ego sent her the message: *He wants you.*

The next day, Amy's friend Stephanie told her that Chad already had a girlfriend. Upset, Amy decided to put Chad out of her mind. But Chad kept showing up, and Amy's ego liked all the attention. Amy knew that Chad had a girlfriend, but she didn't mention it.

Chad pressured her to have sex with him. Amy didn't really want to, but ended up doing it anyway. After having sex, Chad told Amy that he had a girlfriend. At that moment, Amy realized that she had been used. Chad didn't want Amy as a girlfriend; he just wanted sex.

Amy felt betrayed, but who *really* betrayed Amy?

Egomaniacs do things for all the wrong reasons.

Amy created a karmic debt by not being true to herself. Her ego said yes to sex with Chad, even though her feelings said no. Amy knew Chad was deceitful when she learned about his girlfriend, but she bypassed her better judgment for ego gratification. Amy may have experienced an

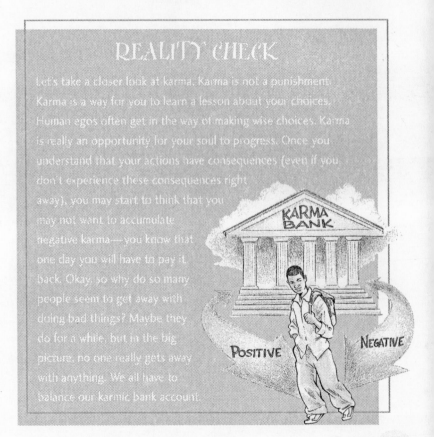

REALITY CHECK

Let's take a closer look at karma. Karma is not a punishment. Karma is a way for you to learn a lesson about your choices. Human egos often get in the way of making wise choices. Karma is really an opportunity for your soul to progress. Once you understand that your actions have consequences (even if you don't experience these consequences right away), you may start to think that you may not want to accumulate negative karma—you know that one day you will have to pay it back. Okay, so why do so many people seem to get away with doing bad things? Maybe they do for a while, but in the big picture, no one really gets away with anything. We all have to balance our karmic bank account.

instant balance of her karma when Chad ditched her and went back to Cathy. Her hurt and embarrassment were payback enough for selling herself short.

Let's balance positive karma against negative karma. List your actions according to each side.

POSITIVE KARMA	NEGATIVE KARMA
Helped a friend with history.	Lied to parents about doing chores.
Volunteered at a soup kitchen.	Spread a negative rumor about a classmate.

Keep adding to your lists. Check to see if one list is longer than the other.

Your karma is strictly your own creation.

Many times I tell people, "You create your own heaven or hell right here on earth by your thoughts, words, and actions." When you die, your spirit body leaves your earthly body and goes back home to the spirit realm, which we call heaven. That heaven is shaped by the choices you made during your earthly life.

So, if you attempt to live a decent life on earth by respecting yourself and others, you will gravitate to a heaven that is filled with peace, joy, and love. You will connect with others who are like you and want to live harmoniously with one another. It's as if you become members of a celestial symphony in tune with one another.

Heaven is not a place, but a very vivid state of mind.

We all have different views of what heaven is. Much of this is learned through our particular religious belief system. A popular view is that heaven is filled with winged angels playing harps, floating in a city made of clouds. My view of heaven comes from the thousands of conversations I have had with those who have passed over into the heavenly realms. I have been told that heaven is a reflection of a spirit's life achievements as well as its wrongdoings while on earth. There are as many levels of spiritual regions, or heaven, as there are mind-sets among people.

When I speak to a spirit who has just left the earthly plane and is newly arrived in the spiritual plane, I can tell. Its thoughts come to me in a very urgent, highly emotional manner, and its personality traits are very clear to me. When a spirit being has been in the spirit world for a longer time, it usually communicates quite differently. The thoughts

James Van Praagh

will be calm, clear, and easy for me to understand. It will communicate in a more loving and
meaningful way to its loved one on earth.

The Big Picture

Most of us journey through life totally
unaware of its spiritual dimensions.

In heaven we have a better view of the big picture of life and our role in it. I often tell people that while you are on earth, you are
walking around with sunglasses on and when
you return home to heaven, you take them off.
In the spirit realms, you are able to see much
more clearly. Spirits refer to us on earth as the
"walking dead," because most of us go through
life totally unaware of its spiritual dimensions.

Everything you do on earth is connected to heaven. Essentially,
heaven is above, around, and below you. Its energy vibrates at a much
higher frequency than we can see, hear, or touch, but we always have
one foot in the door.

That foot is your spirit body, and it lives in heaven all the time.
Whoa! How can you be in two places at one time? You can because you
and your soul aren't in different places *physically*, but *dimensionally*. The
universe is multidimensional and every dimension vibrates at a differ-

ent frequency. You are a multidimensional being because your human body houses your spirit body, and your spirit body is not limited by dimensions of time, space, or form. As you grow spiritually, you become more perceptive of these other dimensions.

The first and most important lesson you learn in heaven is that you never die. There is *no death*! You are immortal. Out of all the things you collect on this earth, like your car, CDs, or clothes, the only thing you take when you leave is the love that you gave to others and to yourself. So . . . a lot of the lessons on this earth are lessons about love . . . love for yourself, your family, your friends, and even people you don't know.

'The only thing you take is love'

James Van Praagh

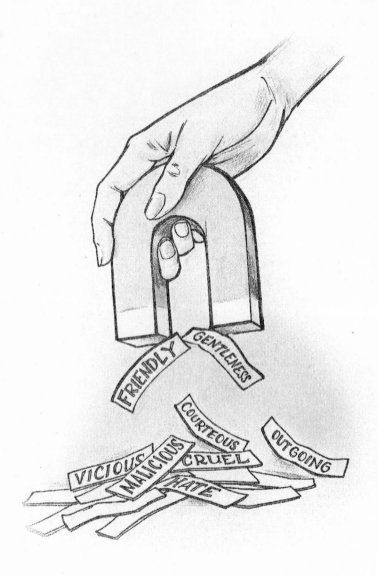

Think of It and Presto, It's Yours!

The Magic of Your Mind

Your Mind Is Filled with a Lot of Info

Question: With all that's going on around us, how do we remember that we are spirits living in a physical world?

Answer: Okay, so it is not always easy to remember the real you when there are so many distractions and material goodies to contend with. Sometimes it feels as if we are living inside a Nintendo game because everything is moving so fast. We are constantly being bombarded by sounds and images from all sides. With all the choices, which one is best for you?

Just imagine what it would be like if you could use TV or Nintendo to help you understand what's going on in your life instead of allowing it to fill your mind with a lot of car crashes and body blows.

You *can*! You have a powerful tool right there inside you, and it's called your mind. It's even quicker than clicking TV or playing Nintendo, and it stores more information than you can possibly imagine.

All you have to do is learn how to use it correctly. The best part is that only you have the power to control what goes in and out of your mind—which means that you can figure out how to do something in your life or change what you don't like.

The Magnetic Field Around You

When I was a kid, I was fascinated by magnets. It amazed me how those metal bits and pieces could be scooped up by a magnet while other things would not be affected at all. I understood that some sort of electromagnetic force in the magnet was attracted to the electromagnetic force in the metal. That's why magnets stick to refrigerator doors, which are metal and have electromagnetic energy running through them, and not to wood cabinets or plastic, things that have no electromagnetism.

The idea of electromagnetic energy attracting other electromagnetic energy is similar to a universal law called the law of affinity, or "like attracts like." We attract to us what is like us, much like a magnet attracts other magnetic material.

For example, if you are typically a good-natured person, you will be around things that reflect that good nature. If you are unhappy or disappointed or down in the dumps, you will find yourself surrounded by people and experiencing situations that reflect those feelings. You attract what is similar to the way you think and feel. That is why it's hard to change your situation without changing your thinking and feeling patterns first.

For instance, the biggest complaint I hear from people is about not having enough money. When opportunities arise and you don't have money, it's common to think, I don't have money to do that. I am broke. Guess what? Thinking that way doesn't solve anything—you still don't have money! That kind of negative thinking and feeling usually attracts situations and circumstances where you don't have enough and can't get anything, either. In turn, these situations continue to reinforce your belief that you lack greenbacks and are always without stuff.

Self-Fulfilling Prophecy

Think of your mind as one giant computer. Whatever you program into your computer generally works, one way or another. Let's put it another way: if it's not in the program, you're not going to pull it up on the screen and be able to do what you want to do. The same thing happens when you put all that stuff you think about day and night into your mind. You create a mental program that will do only what you have told it to do.

Here's yet another way to put it. Think of yourself as a human radio station. You are constantly sending out and receiving signals with your thoughts. If you are thinking things like,

I am always messing up.
There must be something wrong
**   with me.**
I don't like the way I look.
Everyone is out to get me.
I am always getting my
**   parents upset.**
I hate school.
I'm so sick of the way boys/
**   girls act.**
Everything is so unfair.

You tune in to the words that play over and over in your head, like hearing the same old station playing the same old song. Do you expect these tired, downbeat thoughts to change your life into something wonderful? I'm sorry to say it doesn't work that way. These thoughts travel unseen through the atmosphere and create a world of self-fulfilling prophecy.

Cindy, for example, was a friend in high school who was always complaining. "Nobody understands me" was her standard line when anything went wrong in her life. When papers she had written came back to her, she would show me all the remarks written in red by the teacher: "What does this mean?" Or, "I don't get it. Be more clear!" When we were out with a group of friends and she made a comment, someone would often turn around and say, "Cindy, what are you trying to say?"

Feedback like this only reinforced Cindy's belief that she was completely misunderstood and couldn't do a thing about it. Even I began to believe that she might be right—nobody did understand her.

Then I realized what the trouble was. Cindy would talk around things and never get to the point, and people listening to her had to think too hard to understand her point of view. She would go on and on, and people literally tuned her out.

I didn't know it at the time, but Cindy's thinking affected the way she presented herself to the world, creating a vicious cycle. The more Cindy thought no one understood her, the more she'd try to explain in her confusing way, and the more no one did understand her. She had to change that one thought of "nobody understands me" to something like "I make my point clearly" in order to change the energy pattern she had created around herself.

Thoughts are very subtle because they vibrate at a high frequency. However, they are very real, even if we can't see them. They create very real and powerful feelings and experiences. Your whole life up to now is the result of the thoughts you have been thinking. So, what kind of thoughts are they?

You get what you give.

What If?

When I first moved to Los Angeles, I rode the bus to work because I didn't have a car. Waiting for a bus in LA, though, was like waiting for a spaceship to land: there was never one in sight. It definitely got worse in the pouring rain, too, when all the streets flooded and the mud came down from the hillsides right on top of my shoes. A car would have made things so much easier. This really sucks, I used to think. How can I get a car if I can't really afford one?

Since that train of thought wasn't getting me a new car, I decided to play a different scenario in my head. I began to visualize myself driving a beautiful two-seater convertible. That was the classy way to get around La-La Land. I saw every detail of the car, including the leather seats and the wood detail on the dash. I felt pretty good sitting in that car driving down the Sunset Strip. It was a beautiful daydream.

A few months later, a friend of a friend was taking a trip to Hawaii and needed someone to watch his house. I volunteered my services because not only was it a chance to live in a nice house, but it paid as well. After a few days at my temporary living quarters, I received a phone call from the owner of the house, telling me that he'd decided to stay in Hawaii and was going to sell his home. I volunteered my time to help him make arrangements to show his home and keep it looking nice for prospective buyers. I also made arrangements to have his stuff moved out. He appreciated my help. When I told him how much it would cost to have his car transported to Hawaii, he decided it wasn't worth the expense.

"You keep it for helping me out," he said.

"Who, me?" I replied in complete surprise.

There in the garage was the car of my dreams. It was a two-seater Spider convertible. It had tons of miles, but who cared? It was exactly what I wanted.

So how do you believe something that is the total opposite of your experience? You change your negative "what ifs" to positive ones. . . .

> ◎ **Instead of . . . What if she doesn't like me and turns me down for a date?**

You change to . . .

> ◎ **What if I get a date with the girl in civics class because she thinks I'm cool?**

Instead of . . .

> ◎ **What if I don't pass my math test and have to repeat the course?**

You change to . . .

> ◎ **What if I do well on my math test and get into the college I want?**

Instead of . . .

> ◎ **What if I look like a fool when I'm giving my report?**

You change to . . .

> ◎ **What if I get a lot of attention when I ace that oral exam?**

Just because we're not used to talking to ourselves in a positive way doesn't mean we can't. Practice a new way of self-talk and you'll find that it will get easier as time goes by.

The more you think of getting what you want, the more likely you are to get it. But you have to stick to it. You can't think it once, then the rest of the day go back to "I can't," "I don't," or "I'm never going to." In order to magnetize what you want, you will have to think it is coming to you. Your thoughts and feelings will begin to attract that which you say you want. *Like attracts like.*

Signpost #3: The key to success is your imagination.

REALITY CHECK

Every day we pass through a sea of invisible but powerful thoughts. Thoughts always reflect the nature of the person who gives them life. Look closely at the people you hang out with. Their thoughts affect you, just as yours affect them. If there is a dominant personality among the crowd, that person's energy can overcome yours and you can buy into ideas that may not be best for you. Be aware of the thoughts and feelings you have when you are around this person. If they are tearing you down rather than building you up, you have the power to change the situation. First, you can walk away from the situation. Second, you can learn to build self-confidence. Third, think positively about yourself so you will feel more self-reliant. When you do these things, you will be a lot less vulnerable to another person's dominant energy.

MS. SMITH IS SO UGLY, SHE MAKES MY WORN-OUT SHOES LOOK GOOD.

Write the thoughts most often on your mind. If they are negative, stop for a minute and decide to change them. You may not believe your new, positive thoughts, and it may take a while for your thinking to change totally, but hang in there. Here are some examples to help you start.

OLD THOUGHTS	NEW THOUGHTS
I hate the way I look. Why don't I have a body like J.Lo?	Every day I feel better about my looks. I am beautiful inside and out.
Why can't I do better in sports?	I am strong and powerful on the football field. I see myself winning the game and everyone cheering me on.
I am sick of doing homework.	I release all resistance to doing my homework. I know that the more I learn, the more interesting I become to others.
I'm going to do it to them before they do it to me.	No one is against me. Everyone is a potential friend.
I wish I didn't have to live at home.	My home is a peaceful haven. I live in harmony with others and contribute to the harmony in my home.

Your turn . . .

_____   _____

_____   _____

_____   _____

_____   _____

_____   _____

What Do You Believe?

An accumulation of thoughts become beliefs, and these beliefs become a mental state of being. As you grow up, you accumulate a lot of beliefs from your parents, who got their beliefs from their parents, and so on and so forth. But what may have been a good belief a hundred years ago may not work in today's universe.

James Van Praagh

Too often, beliefs cause separation and resentment among people. Beliefs are based on the conditions of the material world. They are different according to where you grow up—what you learned to believe may be very different from what I learned. Beliefs can either be roadblocks or roadways. A variety of beliefs can make life interesting and colorful. Trouble only happens when I want you to believe the way I do and you want me to believe the way you do. Instead of defending our beliefs and excluding or denigrating others, we can integrate them all and live harmoniously. It would be so absolutely dull if we all believed in the same thing, wouldn't it?

On this topic, two buddies come to mind. While their beliefs about schoolwork and outside activities differed, they were the best of friends. Clay always had his nose stuck in a book, while Scott never seemed to take a book home at all. He was more involved in extracurricular activities, which included volunteering in the Big Brother program. He always seemed to be finished with his homework before he left school. I must admit, he made it look easy. Clay, on the other hand, made studying look like a chore, and he wasn't interested in anything outside of school. These two guys had two opposite belief systems going on, but they were both A students. So you see, two different roads can still get you to the same place.

Have you ever seen those billboards for Apple Computer? THINK DIFFERENT, they read.

That's what you've got to do.

Even if you have bought into other people's beliefs, learned some behavior that doesn't really work for you, and maybe picked up some

Don't believe what others say, find out for yourself.

bad habits like smoking, doing drugs, and drinking alcohol, you can always change and think different.

Believe in Yourself

Close your eyes for a moment. See yourself sitting in your classroom. See yourself smiling. You can understand everything the teacher is saying. Next, see yourself leaving school. You have many friends around you. You are all laughing and having a good time. You feel appreciated for who you are. The sun is shining on you and you feel warm and very relaxed all over. Every day, the light from the sun is filling your mind with wisdom and knowledge. With each breath you take, you feel confident and prepared. No matter what comes your way today, you can handle it.

Take a nice, deep breath and open your eyes.

If you believe anything, believe in yourself and the power you possess as a spiritual being.

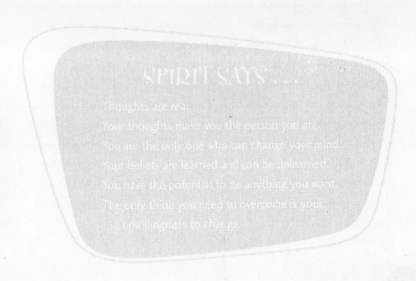

SPIRIT SAYS . . .

Thoughts are real.
Your thoughts make you the person you are.
You are the only one who can change your mind.
Your beliefs are learned and can be unlearned.
You have the potential to be anything you want.
The only thing you need to overcome is your
unwillingness to change.

I Know What I Know, and That's That

Tap into Your Sixth Sense

I Had a Hunch It Was You

We know what our five senses are—sight, hearing, taste, touch, and smell. But we have another sense that is equally as real as the other five. Often referred to as our sixth sense, psychic ability, or our intuition, is the gut feeling or hunch you have that you cannot logically explain.

All of us use this sixth sense every day without even knowing it. For instance, have you ever thought of a friend, and the next minute, the phone rings, and there on the other end is your friend calling? Or you suddenly walk down a street that you never take on your way home, and there in a store window is the sweater you have been searching for? How many times have you been thinking of a particular song, and the next tune you hear on the radio is the same one? These are all intuitive experiences.

Where does this sixth sense come from? In Greek, the word *psychic* means "of the soul." When we use our intuition, our psychic sense, we are tuning in to the energy of the soul. As I said, the soul has a memory with a lot of information stored inside. This inner knowingness is as reliable as your other five senses.

That Funny Feeling

Like it was for most teens, hanging out with my friends on the weekends was a regular routine for me. We used to bike over to a vacant lot and meet to plan what we wanted to do. One particular Saturday, we decided to go to a nearby pond. On our way, we stopped for a red light at a busy intersection. When the light turned green, my friends raced across the street, but I could not move. My feet felt as if they were glued to the pedals. Then I had this funny feeling inside my stomach.

On the other side, my friends shouted, "Hurry up or you'll miss the light." The more I tried to pedal, the more my feet kept slipping. The light turned red again, and I was stuck there.

Suddenly, an old man began to walk into the street against the light, totally unaware of oncoming traffic. I dropped my bike and ran after him, to pull him back on the curb. The old man looked at me with a startled expression, and then realized what I had done. He thanked me over and over again. I just nodded, got back on my bike, and whizzed away to join my friends.

I didn't know it at the time, but this experience was an intuitive encounter. Like many funny feelings I got back then, it was a message of some sort, only I had no idea what. Nor did I understand exactly where they were coming from. Intuition? The only time I ever heard the word was when my father said something about my mother's intuition.

Still, it was hard not to pay attention to these feelings. First, I would get a jittery sensation in my stomach, then a quick chill shot through my body, all of it completely spontaneous. Usually, I forgot about these funny feelings or explained them away with some rationale or another.

After all, I wanted to do all the things other kids did—play sports, meet girls, and have fun. It was not until I was an adult that I began to explore this sixth sense.

Signpost #4: Trust your hunches.

Exploring Psychic Phenomena

How did I begin my exploration? I read a lot of books on psychic development. They contained a variety of techniques and exercises to help me relax and become sensitive to my intuition. At first, it was a hit-or-miss situation because my head always wanted to tell me what to do. Eventually, though, I became very good at listening to that inner knowing.

When I first started working on my intuition, I experimented with my coworkers, trying to guess things like how many people would show up for our weekly staff meetings. I would arrange the chairs ahead of time according to the number of people I felt would attend. When my coworkers walked into the room, they all shook their heads in concert, as if to say, "Oh, God—another one of Van Praagh's psychic tricks."

At one particular meeting, I set out twenty-four chairs, but only twenty-two people showed up. My friend Jodie looked over to me and winked. "Sorry," she whispered.

Then, five minutes after the meeting started, our supervisor walked in with two new employees and introduced them to the rest of the staff. I winked back at Jodie and whispered, "Told you so."

My psychic games always had people talking. The hardest thing for me to learn was not to be afraid of what others thought, even if they thought I was a nut.

As I got better at trusting my instincts, my psychic ability grew. One day, my supervisor asked if I wanted to go with her to see Brian Hurst, a medium. I had no idea what a medium was, but I jumped at the chance to leave the mail room and discover something new.

We met Brian in his home, and he seemed a little too pleasant for his line of work: my mind raced with images of demons and sorcery. Nevertheless, I settled into one of his couches and went along with the wild ride.

For the next hour, Brian contacted friends and relatives who had passed into the spirit world for the people in the room. At the end of the session, he turned to me and said, "You know, James, you have the gift yourself. The spirit beings are telling me that one day you will give readings just like this to other people. The spirits are planning to use you."

I wasn't sure what to say. "I have enough trouble understanding the living," I answered. "Why would I want to start talking to the dead?"

He just smiled. "One day you will."

After that experience, more and more people at work came to me to ask about their lives. I was getting a high from just having my intuitive impressions verified. It showed me that learning to trust my feelings and hunches was valuable and could help me in my everyday interactions with people. Eventually, I developed my intuitive ability more intensely through meditation and group gatherings until one day, I had the courage to quit my job and become a full-time medium, just as Brian had predicted.

Following your intuition may not be the logical choice.

Another term for intuition is *gut feeling*. Have you ever felt something in your heart that you *had* to do? Something that on second thought you didn't do because you were afraid to be wrong or look dumb? On the other hand, have you had a definite urge to do something, and despite others' tries to discourage you from doing it, felt so strongly about it that you did it anyway?—and had it turn out to be right on?

We are all taught to mask our true feelings. People are afraid of the unknown, and our feelings, our intuition, is often illogical and therefore unknown and unknowable. But when you hold back what you are really feeling, you become frustrated and lose confidence in yourself. You become a follower, not a leader.

The feelings I had as a young boy, those jitters and chills I tried to shrug off, are not the same as everyday emotional ups and downs. Don't confuse your intuition with your emotions. Feelings like happiness, sadness, anger, and loneliness come from social interaction, your own personality, and your bodily hormones. Because of that, these emotions will change from one moment to another.

The gut feelings I am talking about are instinctive and come from a part of your unconscious mind. They are not reactions to what somebody else says or does, and they are not brought on by hormonal changes in your body. Your intuition is a very subtle sense, but you can learn to become very aware of it.

Wishing It Were So Doesn't Make It So

It's hard to pay attention to your gut feeling because your mind has a logical answer for almost everything. We talk ourselves in and out of things a million times a day. I tell my audience, "Go with your first impression."

On the other hand, we can often get caught up in a wishful-thinking syndrome. It goes like this: you wish so hard for something that you think it must be your heart, or your gut, leading you in the right direction. That's not necessarily the case, though. Our wishes can be twisted by judgments, opinions, or a desire for someone or something.

I remember Michelle, a friend of mine in high school who had a mad crush on a guy. She was very shy, but she was so infatuated that she joined the drama group just to be near him. He was a senior and a lead actor in the group. Michelle was a freshman and signed up to learn stage makeup.

"You see, I knew I could get close to him," she said. "I put his makeup on every night just before he goes on stage."

I really wanted Michelle to be happy, but I had my doubts that he was as interested in her as she was in him.

"Jamie, I have a feeling he likes me," she insisted. "He knows my name and says hello in the hallway between classes. It gives me the shivers just to think about it. I think he'll ask me out soon. Don't you think so?"

Poor Michelle thought she was getting some intuitive feeling about her dream guy, but it was only wishful thinking on her part. Her shivers were something she herself created. The guy never did ask her out. His hellos in the hallway were his way of being polite. After all, they were both in the drama club, and saw each other every night. Michelle's dream guy graduated that year, and she never saw him again.

As Michelle's experience shows, desires are not the same as intuitive feelings. But neither are fears. How many times have you wanted to do something, but your mind said no? It's not going to work, your mind says. Or, Everyone will laugh at this idea, or, Nobody cares. Such messages of disapproval are part of the beliefs that have been programmed into your mind. They are responses you learned from the people around you. Intuition, however, is not a negative response. Although it may feel crazy or awkward or cause you to take a risk, intuition will never lead you to harm.

IS IT YOUR INTUITION? ASK YOURSELF THESE SIMPLE QUESTIONS:

- Is this feeling influenced by my judgment about someone? (Criticism is *not* your intuition.)
- Do I wish it were so? If so, why? (Wishing is *not* your gut feeling.)
- Am I rationalizing what just came to mind? (Logic is *not* intuition.)

Meditation:
Learning How to Tune In to Yourself

The first way to start getting in touch with your intuition is through a daily practice of meditation. Meditation is the key to developing your sixth sense. When people hear the word *meditation,* they think of sitting cross-legged on the floor, with incense burning and low voices chanting. Quite right. This is a form of meditation.

But meditation has many forms. Prayer, for instance, is a type of meditation. When you pray, you focus on something internal rather than external. Other forms of meditation do not require you to sit still. Painting, writing, studying, dancing, exercising, even playing computer games fall into this category. What they all have in common is that they are different approaches to a meditative process whereby your mind is so focused on something that you block out everything else going on around you.

The meditation process I recommend throughout this book is the sitting-still kind that you do for about twenty minutes a day. All I can say is that meditation time is important time to spend with yourself. Here are some of my step-by-step guidelines.

1. Set aside a special place for your meditation process. Pick a corner of your room where you can practice and not be disturbed. Get rid of all the junk in that corner so you can feel that this place is your special place.

2. Turn off your phone, cell phone, pager, computer, and answering machine, and anything else that could distract you.

3. If you like, you can light a candle and play some relaxing music. Try to select something that will calm rather than excite you.

4. Sit on the floor or in a chair, and make sure you are comfortable but not slouched over. Your back should be straight so that the energy can move up and down your spine. Keep your arms rested on your legs and not crossed over your body.
   Try not to fall asleep.

5. Close your eyes and begin to relax. Think of your arms and legs as totally relaxed, like wet noodles. All the stress of your day leaves your body during these few moments. You will get back to your stuff when you are finished meditating.

6. Concentrate on your breathing. This is an important part of meditation. When you first start out, you may find it hard to sit still and breathe. But keep at it until you can feel yourself relaxing with each breath. Think of your breath as everything. Without it, you cannot live.

7. Your meditation may be as easy as breathing in and out, or you may want to do a visualization, as described in the next few paragraphs.

Meditate to Develop Intuition

The following are some guidelines for learning how to tune in to your intuition. Go to your meditation place and begin with the deep breathing process.

When you are relaxed, visualize your breath coming into your body like a stream of golden light, which then fills every organ, cell, and muscle of your body. As you exhale, see a gray mist exit your body. This represents all excess energy, anxiety, fear, and stress you may have. With each exhalation, you will feel lighter as you free yourself of these heavy energies.

Now imagine your whole body being filled with golden light. Continue to breathe until you feel bathed in this golden light. You can sit there for a few minutes in the stillness of your own energy.

When you feel finished, open your eyes. In the beginning you may only be able to sit for five minutes. Eventually you will be able to practice for a full twenty minutes. The more you are able to relax and medi-

The more you use intuition, the stronger it becomes.

James Van Praagh   47

tate, the more you rid the mind of extraneous clutter, and the easier your intuition can come through.

You Have the Answer

Sometimes it seems a lot easier to listen to other people's opinions than to listen to yourself. Following your intuition is listening to yourself for the answers. If you have to make a decision about something, such as a new relationship or which college is best for you, sit down in your meditation place, clear your mind of all preconceived ideas, and ask yourself, "What's the right choice for me right now?"

At first, your emotions may come up, or you may raise some judgmental thoughts. These are probably the things you've felt and heard from other people. Let them go and tune in to what you think. Learning to listen to yourself and your own soul information takes practice. Learn to do it now. It will help you a lot as you get older and have more and more choices to make. Begin now to learn to trust yourself.

James Van Praagh

Everyone Is in Your Life for You

Meeting Your Soulmates and Spirit Guides

Get on the Soul Train

One of the questions I am asked frequently is, "Do I have a soulmate?"

My answer is absolutely YES!

You don't have *one* soulmate; you have *many* soulmates in one lifetime. Pretty exciting stuff.

Soulmates are very much like your best friends. You like to hang out with them. When you come back to earth to learn some more, you ask some of your soulmates to come too, so you can share the lessons together. The people in your life now, like your parents, siblings, classmates, cousins, friends, and even teachers are souls with whom you have shared your life before. You all come back to grow and learn together. This is your soul group, and each one of these people is a soulmate.

The idea that you will have only one soulmate in your lifetime is pure fantasy. It's nice to know that you have many soulmates in the world, some you haven't even met yet.

Life is a mystery, and each day you unravel it a little more. With each new person you meet, you are being told something about your purpose in life and what you are here to learn. So, everyone in your life is here for a reason; they're here for *you*.

SUPPORT YOUR FAMILY SOUL TEAM

Having the Home-Court Advantage

Okay, so you're in a soul group. You picked all these people to be with you . . . even your parents. Whenever I tell an audience that they picked their parents, I hear a loud groan. "Oh, God, not me. I would *never* pick these people for my parents."

You picked your parents because you are supposed to be with them. Still can't believe it?

Someone said to me at one of my demonstrations, "Why on earth would I pick a father who is always angry when I could have someone rich, famous, or who at least treats me like my best friend?"

It's really hard to say to someone, or even yourself, that your abusive mother or alcoholic father is in your life because you picked her or him. Sometimes, though, we pick a difficult parent to learn how not to be like him or her. On a soul level, you always pick others to learn something

Signpost #5: You are in a situation to learn something.

about yourself. Many times, you want to be with certain people again just because you love them: a parent in this life, for example, may have been a sister in another. The ups and downs of daily life are ways you fulfill your karmic ties with each other.

This doesn't mean that you have to stay stuck in your nightmare. Maybe your task in this lifetime is to develop inner strength and confidence or to learn how to rely on yourself.

Getting Left Behind

Growth is never easy and is accomplished only by experiencing every aspect of a situation until you "get it." We learn best from difficult situations, and we all get ample opportunities to mess up and do it over again.

James Van Praagh

A teen by the name of Jane came to my office many years ago along with her father. Immediately, I could see a lot of dark colors around her. I could also feel a heaviness as she entered the room.

I said to Jane, "You're hanging out with a very bad crowd, and you must leave them right away."

Jane was annoyed to hear this. I could sense that she was very vulnerable and easily swayed by other people's opinions.

"They are my friends. I can't live without them," she said defiantly.

I understood Jane's need to be part of the group. Sometimes, we give up a lot of ourselves just to be with certain people, so we can feel wanted.

"These kids are bad for you," I said. "Their energy is destructive and hateful. They will pull you down to their level."

Jane's father was totally unaware of this piece of news. He told Jane that she could no longer go out with these friends, and he made her promise that she would obey.

I felt that Jane needed some more subtle coaxing, so I suggested some ways she could feel stronger and more self-confident.

"Begin each day by closing your eyes and imagining the sun shining over you, filling you with its warmth and light. Say these words: I am the light of God. Say these words whenever your friends want you to do something you don't want to do. The more you practice, the stronger you will feel."

HURRY IN, WE GOTTA GO!

Jane seemed very reluctant to get out of her rut.

Two years later, I learned that she had been killed in a car crash. The driver was one of the friends Jane thought she couldn't live without. The friend died, too, drunk at the wheel.

Even though we may have some bad karmic ties with people,

we always have free will to choose a different course of action than the one we are headed on. Jane could have left her friends and would have gotten over it in time. She knew in her heart that these people were dangerous. In fact, she may have had very similar karmic ties with them in a previous life, and this life was her opportunity to learn how to get rid of their stranglehold over her. Instead, she repeated the same pattern with the same group of souls just like getting left behind when you fail in school. She will have another chance to take the class over and change this pattern of low self-worth, insecurity, and anxiety to one of self-confidence and self-reliance in a future life, perhaps with the same soulmates.

You can change what you don't want, even your friends.

Your friends are part of your soul group. Write the qualities you want in your friends.

_____

_____

_____

What qualities do you have to offer your friends? Are they similar to the ones you want in them?

_____

_____

_____

James Van Praagh

Which qualities do you feel come from your soul experiences of lifetimes shared with your friends?

_____

_____

_____

Can you feel it when a person has been with you before? Make a list of qualities that let you know you have been together sharing a life before.

_____

_____

_____

Do you find negative qualities in yourself and friends that are similar?

_____

_____

_____

When You Meet Your True Love

I am often asked, "James, is there someone I am meant to be with? Do I have one true soulmate?"

Yes, we do have loves from previous lifetimes that we want to perpetuate this time around.

The boyfriends and girlfriends to whom you are drawn at this time in your life could be the one—or one of many loves you will have.

As with any soulmate, you connect with him or her so that both of you can fulfill your soul contract together. Soul contracts are made with

our soulmates before we come to earth. We both agree to share a certain
type of experience with each other.

This is the one, you sometimes think, but after a while one person
wants to stay in the relationship and the other wants to move on, so you
break up. Sometimes you think it's the end of the world. It's not. You
don't have to feel like a loser.

What is really happening?

Usually the end of a relationship means that the soul contract between two people has been completed. That's why I tell people not to
panic. No one comes into your life by mistake. And yes, you will get another opportunity to meet a soulmate, perhaps the one you are meant to
be with for the rest of your life.

James Van Praagh

Spiritual Soulmates

In addition to the soulmates we have in the people around us, we also have invisible soulmates. They are our spiritual helpers. I call them spirit guides because they intervene for us and assist us in our earthly missions. There are many types of guides, and to me, guardian angels and guides are one and the same.

Before we are born, we meet with some of our spirit guides in the spirit realm. These guides could be highly evolved beings who may or may not have lived on earth, or familiar persons, like relatives or friends, whom we have known in previous lifetimes. These spiritual soulmates help us to choose our curriculum and classes for our upcoming lifetime on earth. They assist us in understanding ourselves so we can make the right choices for our spiritual development.

Spirit guides also want to learn and evolve. Like us, highly evolved beings are on a path to perfection. They participate in our lives so that they can learn from a particular experience to become better guides. So everyone gets what they want.

Discovering My Master Guides

Spirit guides come to us in many forms. The first comprises our master teachers. These guides may appear to us as religious persons or saints. Others may appear as mythological characters or authority figures. I have several master guides who work with me.

When I was in England, a gifted psychic by the name of Irene Martin-Giles told me that a Chinese man named Chang was my spiritual teacher. Chang was in my life to help in the delivery of messages from the spirit world. Irene began to draw a picture of the spirit she saw in her mind's eye. He was dressed in a long blue robe and wore an orange-and-blue beanie on his head. It was the kind of cap quite prevalent in China during the early 1900s. Chang had a long, narrow face and brown eyes. In the center of his robe was a ten-pointed star, and in the middle of the star was a green jewel. He was surrounded by a golden light that marked him as a master from a very high spiritual plane. Many times a guide will dress in a style from a period of time that is particularly representative of his or her tradition. When I first saw Master Chang's face in my mind's eye, I felt a loving attraction to it.

Another master guide appeared quite unexpectedly during a séance. At this séance, I fell into a trance so I don't remember what happened. Luckily, someone in the group taped the session, and played back the tape to me afterward. I was astounded when I heard my own voice, speaking in a very distinctive British accent! The spirit speaking through me, I learned, was Harry Aldrich, a British doctor with a very authoritarian personality. He had lived in London and had passed over some time in the 1930s. One of the ways Dr. Aldrich helps me is by identifying physical ailments that my clients may have.

Most of us will have one or two master teachers who stay with us

REALITY CHECK

Let's take a closer look at what I mean by séance. A séance is a circle of people who want to tune in to the spirit world and contact spirit beings that have passed over. Usually, a medium, like myself, leads a séance, because there must be someone in charge who is able to communicate with spirits by seeing, hearing, or feeling their energy. A medium is also aware of the kind of spirit beings that are not for the group's highest good, the kind that may want to zap energy from those involved.

James Van Praagh

throughout our soul's evolution, lifetime after lifetime. Sometimes, we have a master teacher to guide us through a particular lifetime. Based on our soul's evolution, a guide is drawn to us when a certain lesson or aspect of our personality, such as patience or humility, needs to be perfected.

Personal and Specialty Guides

The next group of spirit guides are personal guides. These are persons we have known in other lifetimes or relatives and friends who have passed over in this lifetime.

My grandmother and I shared a close relationship when I was growing up. I have a lot of favorite memories of the two of us spending our Saturdays together. Now that she has passed over, she often comes to me in my dreams. When I wake up from a dream with my grandmother, I always feel safe and assured that she is watching over me.

My mother is also one of my guides. She died a few years ago. We were always very close. Mom was the only one to whom I could express my psychic abilities. When she tries to contact me, she usually does so in a humorous way. Whenever I think of her doing something funny, such as speaking with an Irish brogue like she often did when I was a child, I know she is around. Sometimes she communicates in ways that are uniquely hers. We all know someone about whom we say, "Only so and so could do it that way!" Well, that's my mom.

I remember being lost on a trip in Italy. I couldn't read the map because it was in Italian! So I kept going around and around in circles, getting nowhere. Suddenly, a truck came zooming down this narrow two-lane highway. Emblazoned across the truck's side was REGINA. I knew right away it was a sign from Mom, so I followed the truck and reached my destination. How did I know it was a sign? My mother's name was Regina!

Personal guides make attempts to impress us with the best solution for a situation. However, they will never interfere with our choices.

Guides help us to live up
to our potential.

Sometimes, a guide can only stand by and watch us make our decisions, right or wrong as the case may be.

The third category of spirit guides are specialty helpers. These spirit guides come in and out of our lives based on our activities. Some stay for years, while others stay for only a short time. These guides possess certain skills and knowledge, and they encourage us to use our talents in ways to better humanity. For instance, if you want to be a writer or a musician or a scientist, a spirit guide who specializes in these areas of interest will come into your life for however long you need him or her.

Spirit guides are always with us, so you are never really alone. And although our guides may change from time to time, we don't have to call them because they know our needs and are always ready to lend us a helping hand.

Last but not least, there are spiritual guides who are very visible to us. These guides are alive and well and probably around you right now. A teacher could be one of your guides. So could relatives like your aunts and uncles. Brothers and sisters, too! Maybe you have a stepparent who is your guide. Some guides even come disguised as our pets!

James Van Praagh   61

Guides can be pretty ingenious when they want to give us information. They know what we need, even if we don't. The way they let us know is through our intuition. Their messages are subtle and gentle, and often come in the form of hunches. Your guide is not going to blow a horn and make an announcement. That's why I say go with your feelings.

Say, for instance, that you want to get a part-time job after school. You go to the place where you wish to work, but the sign on the window says CLOSED. You call the business, but the phone is always busy. You finally get an answer, but you get the run-around from the person on the other end. You start to get a funny feeling that something isn't right with this particular place.

Closed doors, busy signals, and vagueness are subtle clues. Hel-lo! Your guide is trying to tell you something. He or she wants to warn you that something fishy is going on. You have to pay attention for the subtle clues, like a CLOSED sign, busy phone lines, and incompetent personnel. The spirit guide wants you to know that it's not the job for you!

Guides do not give us outright commands—it doesn't work that way. Unfortunately, most of us go through life in a fog and need to be hit over the head with a baseball bat to become aware of what's going on around us.

I know that there are plenty of times when you may feel lonely and isolated even in a room full of people. I just want to reassure you that you are never alone.

If you cannot express yourself to your parents, teachers, or friends, talk to your spirit guides. They are always with you. Take some time to sit quietly, even meditate, and ask your question. You can ask in your mind or even talk out loud.

Spirit guides communicate their answers through our own thoughts. Any thoughts that are negative or fearful or telling you to do something harmful, however, are not thoughts from your spirit guide, but instead probably thoughts you have heard from others, or your own judgmental mind. Just tell those thoughts to go away. Remember that you are in charge of your mind. No one else can have control over it unless you let them. And one more thing: guides will not hurt us or suggest we hurt someone else. They will not force us to do anything.

> **You can follow your guide's direction or not.**

Making the Connection

Here is a meditation to help you connect to your spirit guides. Begin with the deep-breathing process. As you breathe out, let go of your worries and thoughts about what you have to do.

When you are feeling as relaxed as possible, think of a beautiful place where you would like to meet your spirit guide. It could be a garden, or the beach, or on top of a mountain. Use your imagination to fill in as much detail as possible. This area will become your meeting place, where you will come to talk to your guide.

Once you are in this place of peace, use your thoughts to ask your guide to stand in front of you so that you can see him or her. Don't guess about the appearance of your guide or expect your guide to look a certain way. Simply let him or her come. Notice your guide's physical traits, like the color of his eyes or her hair. How is your guide dressed?

Next, in your mind ask your guide some questions. Who are you? How do you work with me? Do you have a message for me?

Be still and let the answers come to you. Your guide may give you a vision or you may hear something in your mind. You may detect a scent or feel a breeze across your face. Keep your focus on love, not fear.

When you feel that you are finished connecting with your guide, you can open your eyes.

As you work with this visualization, your guide will come into your energy field more frequently. The more open you are to your impressions and feelings, the more confident you will become when conferring with your guide. It is simply a matter of being receptive. Don't be afraid to ask for your guide's help at any time. Guides want to help us because they want us to become aware of our own spiritual identity and the spiritual force in all things.

Write down some questions or guidance you would like to ask of your guide. For example:

Help me figure out why my boyfriend dumped me.
What can I do to manage my anger better?
How can I feel more confident at school?

_____

_____

_____

_____

_____

James Van Praagh

See Yourself As You Really Are

You Have Something Unique to Offer

Am I the Only One Who Doesn't Fit In Here?

When I was very young, I used to watch a Christmas special on TV called *Rudolph the Red-Nosed Reindeer*. I loved the part about the toys none of the children wanted to play with. They all lived together on the Island of Misfit Toys. Meanwhile, Hermey, one of Santa's elves, didn't want to make toys; he wanted to be a dentist. Nobody understood that elf—everyone thought he was strange. How could he not like making toys for Santa? He had a different dream, and the rest of the elves thought he was weird.

I related so much to that elf because I never thought I fit in. I saw myself as one of those "misfit toys." Deep inside, I knew I was basically a good kid, just a little bit different.

And while the rest of my friends were watching Casper cartoons, I was actually seeing real ghosts! When I talked about what I felt and people didn't believe me, I didn't care. I had to be me. No one could tell me that what I saw or heard wasn't real, because it was. I had no idea that it took courage to be myself.

I am grateful that my mother helped me to understand that I wasn't a geek, even if she didn't understand my psychic ability herself. Whenever I asked her about my visions, she would say, "Oh, those are God's angels." It made sense to me.

You've Got to Be Yourself

Even though our parents are soulmates who have been with us before, I think it's fair to say that we never fully get why our parents act a certain way. Underneath their rules and restrictions, they want to do what they feel is best for you. You know why? They actually have gone through some of the stuff you're going through right now, so there is something to be said about experience.

At the same time, it would be cool if parents saw you for who you are rather than who they want you to be. Parents forget that you need the space to be yourself. They may not understand what you like or what you like to do. They may not always be there for you. They may not even encourage your creativity or your talents.

Guess what? You have to do it! It's your life. Whatever goes on, you are here to learn, create, and fulfill your potential. Think of every experience, good, bad, or whatever, as another opportunity for you to be aware of who you are and appreciate your own self-worth.

James Van Praagh

When you put other people down, you shut off a variety of resources and possibilities that can help you grow as a spiritual being. When you're the one being dumped on, you can also shut down the resources that might help you because of the chip you're carrying on your shoulder.

Often, I conduct group demonstrations in front of large audiences, where there could be three hundred to one thousand people present at one time. It gets a little hairy because many spirits flood the room, all of them anxious to communicate to their loved ones who have shown up for the demonstration. The spirits with the strongest and clearest communication are usually the ones that get their messages through.

During one demonstration in Atlanta, a spirit stood by the right side of a teen. "May I come to you?" I asked the young man.

I could tell that this teen was shy and awkward, especially now that he had become the center of attention. At first, he kept his head down, but I persisted.

As I walked toward him, I said, "I have someone here who wants to speak with you."

He was reluctant to acknowledge me, but finally said, "Okay."

"He says he is a friend of yours, someone from high school. He is giving me the name Steve."

The young man was taken by surprise. "That's my name."

"Your friend says he's sorry. He says he called you names and pushed you around a lot. He knows now that he was wrong to do that."

I wanted some sort of confirmation from Steve. "Do you understand?" I asked.

Steve just nodded, amazed at what I was telling him.

"You don't feel very good about yourself, he says. That is why he bullied you. Is this true?"

Finally, Steve spoke up. "Yes, he's right."

"He is sorry for making fun of you. He is telling me that you have to feel better about yourself. You need to like who you are. You have a lot to offer, but you run and hide too much. He says he will be looking out for you."

"Why would he do that?"

Steve was embarrassed. I could tell that he was pretty uncomfortable. I ended the communication, saying to him, "Please see me when the demonstration is over."

Steve came by afterward. We sat down on the corner of the stage so we could speak privately.

"I could tell this was very hard for you."

"I'm glad you stopped when you did," said Steve.

"You don't feel very good about yourself, do you?"

"I'm a geek," he blurted out. "Everyone makes fun of me." Steve then told me about his feelings of failure and all his shortcomings. He felt he was ugly—his face was scarred with acne—and a complete washout.

Steve told me about the bully at school. "You kept saying friend, but he wasn't my friend. He was my enemy. He died in a car crash. I was relieved when I heard the news because I knew he couldn't bother me anymore. I really thought he deserved to die. Why would he want to help me now?"

"Your friend wants to make up for the wrong he did. He says he treated you like a loser. He wants you to know that you're not."

I could tell that Steve had a hard time believing me.

"Don't be stubborn," I said. "Be open to new ideas about yourself. Your friend will help you see yourself in a different light. Things are going to change for the better, but you have to let go of your belief that things are always bad for you."

Steve looked at me tentatively.

"Everybody is afraid of change. Just take one step at a time," I continued. "Start seeing yourself as someone who matters. Once you start, it

YOU ARE NEVER ALONE

will have a domino effect. It will get easier. Your friend will be guiding you."

Steve gave a slight sigh of relief.

I gave him one of my meditation tapes. "Find some time to listen to it. You will start to feel more relaxed about yourself."

"Thanks," said Steve. "You're the first person who really knows how I feel."

"Steve, I want you to know that you're never alone. Please remember that."

I heard from Steve about a year later. He told me he took up skateboarding and "bombs the curves" with his friends every weekend.

How do you see yourself? Rate yourself on a scale from 1 to 10, with 1 being a strong "No" answer and 10 showing complete agreement.

- Are you weak?
- Are you afraid?
- Do you feel ugly?
- Are you influenced by what your friends say or what others think?
- Do you base your self-image on what you see on TV or in the movies?
- Do you speak confidently?
- Do you express your true feelings?
- Do you hide behind a mask and show people that everything is okay when it's not?

Signpost #6: How you see yourself defines how others see you.

Playing Those Reruns

Like Steve, many of us think that we can't change the image we have of ourselves, even though we know it's strictly loserville or doesn't fit who we are right now. Why? Because we play some out-of-date programs that may have been put into our minds at the age of three or four. It's time to change some of them, to update our minds. Here is a sampling of the old programs we play over and over again. I'm sure you can add more.

Fear

Doing things differently from others can seem embarrassing or stupid. You are super self-conscious: "People won't like who I am if I act that way." You try to live up to what other people expect of you, and when you don't, you blame yourself for not being a better person.

Failure

You see yourself as a geek or misfit. You feel that you'll never belong. You will always miss the boat. You think things like, "I'm not smart enough," "I make too many mistakes," "I can't do it," "I don't act like them." You see yourself as a loser. You're a round peg in a square hole. You focus on your faults, not your good points or usefulness.

Helplessness

You are the kind who never owns up to anything because nothing is your fault. You wallow in your own self-pity, with thoughts like, "I feel helpless to do anything to change myself," and "Everyone is doing it to me." "Don't look at me, I didn't do it," you say. You like to complain; it's a form of attention. You really don't want to change.

Pain

Life is too hard, and you don't want to do the work. Besides, no one understands you: "I'm not going to do that, that's stupid." "No one gets me." "Am I the only one who sees it's never going to work?" You like to be alone with your misery. You decide it's better to drop out, take drugs, or drink alcohol to soothe your suffering.

Hate

Anger usually feeds your hate. Everyone out there is against you: "It's a dog-eat-dog world." You take your anger out on other people because it gives you a feeling of being in control or superiority. What you really feel is inferior. "I must do it to them before they do it to me."

What is self-image? Have you ever known athletes who practice and practice and don't do well? Yeah, come on, you know some. Practice is only one part of success. Most athletes will tell you that the key ingredient to winning is seeing themselves win! I once saw a television interview with the track star Marion Jones, a five-time Olympic gold medalist. She said she would visualize herself breaking the ribbon at the finish line over and over in her mind before a race. Now *that's* having a good self-image.

What Can I Do to Change My Negative Self-Image?

Every time you hear something or describe something, a picture of it forms in your head. It's as if you're watching a movie. Sometimes the movie is a blockbuster, and sometimes it's a flop. The same thing happens every time you say something or think something about yourself: it becomes an image inside your head that you play over and over. What kind of movie are you watching? Is it something you want to see?

Change your inner pictures. See yourself in a whole new way.

- **Every time the old picture comes to mind, change the channel. See yourself as a spiritual being. Spiritual beings are whole, creative, and perfect.**
- **Imagine your body being filled with positive energy. It takes only a second to see light radiating within you.**

James Van Praagh

This energy will go out from you wherever you go. Other people will feel it, too.

Ask yourself the following questions:

- What is this experience teaching me?
- Is this what I really want?
- What are my strong features?
- How can I use my strengths to turn this problem around?
- What are the things about life that make me happy?

The answers will give you a new picture of yourself and the situation. If you keep asking, "Why is this happening to me?" your negative program will respond, "Because you're stupid," or something like that. But if you ask, "What am I learning from this experience?" you will get a very different answer.

Be willing to let go of all your fixed ideas and beliefs. It takes practice clicking off the old and clicking on the new, but you'll catch on.

Surf your brain for an enhanced self-image.

Here's What Happens When You Have a Bad Picture of Yourself

When you feel lousy about yourself, life seems pretty miserable. You feel stuck in a TV show you hate to watch. How can you have fun when you hate yourself? You start to look in all the wrong places for ways to make yourself feel better, and you usually find something that works. But at what price?

During a visit to San Francisco, I lined up several private appointments to do readings. Before I begin any reading, I meditate and focus my thoughts on the spirit realm. It takes a few minutes. I then say a little prayer, asking for blessings of love and light for the good of all. I can feel the energy shift in the room as spirit beings begin to surround the person for whom I am doing the reading.

One woman I read for was quite anxious to see me and drove several hours from a rural part of the state. I had never met this woman before, nor did I know the reason for her visit. I had no prior information about the events in her life. Yet, within the hour, I had shared some of the most intimate and painful moments of her life. Luckily, she was able to heal some of those painful memories while communicating with her teenaged daughter on the other side.

"I see a young woman here who has the same eyes as you," I told the mother. "I believe she is your daughter."

The woman's eyes widened.

"She is giving me the name Marcie or Marcia. Is this right?"

"Yes," the mother said, her eyes filling with tears.

"Your daughter tells me that she is with a playmate of hers from childhood. Her playmate got hit by a car and died instantly," I continued.

The mother just sat there amazed at what I was telling her.

"Your daughter says that she is happy now and is sorry that she caused you so much heartache when she was in high school."

James Van Praagh

The mother nodded.

"She is telling me she was in a lot of emotional pain."

"Yes, I know she was."

"Your daughter is talking about not knowing herself. She had a terrible self-image. She is mentioning the name Christy. Do you know who she means?" I asked.

I could tell by the look on this woman's face that the mention of Christy made her very uncomfortable.

I continued even though I knew this was difficult for this mother. "She says that Christy was a bad influence on her."

The mother cried out, "My daughter changed so much because of Christy."

"She is telling me she is sorry for not being nicer to you. She is trying to convey that she was weak and not able to fight off Christy's dominating energy. She says that Christy always attracted bad situations into her life. Christy was always mean to people, especially when she took drugs."

The mother told me that Christy had been in trouble with drugs since the age of fourteen.

"Do you know Sam?" I asked.

The mother's face turned pale. After a moment, she replied, "Yes, I understand. I know she didn't mean it. Oh, God."

I relayed her daughter's agonizing regrets. "She says she wasn't herself. Christy made her do it. She says that Christy filled her with terrible lies about this man Sam."

Marcia was sending me visions of all the gory details. I saw the teen waiting behind a bush by an apartment building. When Sam arrived, Marcia took a gun from her purse and pointed it at his head. He turned to run away, but she shot him in cold blood. Then I saw Marcia turning the gun toward her own head and absorbing a blast as she pulled the trigger and killed herself.

"Your daughter knows now how wrong she was. She says it is important to be true to yourself. She is sorry for being weak and letting Christy take control of her. She was doing what Christy wanted. She wished that she loved herself more."

When spirits contact their loved ones on earth, often they are seeking an opportunity to make amends for any wrongdoing or to express the love they were not able to express on earth. Once spirit beings leave the trappings of the physical body and realize that they are very much alive in a more sublime existence, they have a keener understanding of the big picture of life. A spirit being knows clearly the complete history of all its lifetimes, and it begins to examine every experience and moment of the life it recently departed. Certain experiences will be reevaluated to see if they have contributed to its soul growth. That's why spirits seem to know better than when they were on earth.

Marcia's tragedy probably could have been prevented had she loved and respected herself more. She didn't have a good image of herself and because of that, she let her friend control and manipulate her. If Marcia had had a more positive sense of who she was, she may have been able to free herself from Christy's domination.

Most of us don't experience such an intense situation as this one. Still, when you hate who you are, or don't like the way you look, or think of yourself as a loser or a weakling, or are just plain afraid, others can very easily influence you, and sometimes these influences can be dangerous.

Learn to love yourself as you are right now. Each day, your own love will create an energy shield of positive vibrations around you. This will help you let go of negative people and negative experiences, just like water rolling off a duck's back.

Love yourself the way you are!

List the people and things that frighten you or stress you out. Next to each one, write a word or sentence to describe it.

STRESSING POINTS	DESCRIPTION
Sally	She makes me so angry with her gossip.
Homework	I'm not sure of how to do some of the problems.
Prom	No one wants to go with me.
_____	_____
_____	_____
_____	_____
_____	_____

Now, do your breathing meditation. After that, look at your list, and write down a positive alternative to describe each item on your list. Here are some example alternatives:

STRESSING POINTS	ALTERNATIVES
Sally	Tell her I'm not going out with her anymore.
Homework	I need extra help. See if I can get a homework buddy.
Prom	Get a few friends and go together as a group.
_____	_____
_____	_____
_____	_____

Marcia and Steve let other people's opinions dictate how they felt about themselves. They let somebody else push them around because they felt weak and powerless.

We often attract people who mirror and make worse our weak points and negative feelings. I call these types of people psychic vampires. These vampires can transfer their negative energy to us or drain off our energy. Think of sticking a tube in a gas tank and siphoning the gas out: when your energy is siphoned off, you feel vulnerable, discouraged, and out of gas.

The only reason someone can take your energy in the first place is that you are already at a low level. The energy force within you is amazing and awesome, but every day, you give this power away. You want to feel loved, or to be accepted, or to do what is expected of you, so you scatter your energy to this person and that person, this situation and that. By the end of the day, your energy is all over the place.

In such circumstances, it doesn't take much to drain your energy. You call a friend and she unloads her stress on you. You wish you could help her, but you don't know how. Your English test comes back and you barely made a C, just when you were hoping to have a better grade average in English for your college application. Your parents aren't too happy, either. Then, the cute guy you've been dying to date asks you out for Friday—but you promised to baby-sit your neighbor's kids on Friday. By the end of the week, you feel like you're coming down with a cold. There are a lot of people's energy tied into yours. No wonder you feel exhausted. Think of strings go-

ing out from you and connecting to everyone and their problems. That's why there is little left for you. How do you handle this situation?

I remember the time I was a guest on Roseanne's TV talk show. I was already fatigued by a long book tour. Even though I know how to conserve my energy and protect my energy field, I can expose myself to other people's emotional distress. In that studio, when I opened my energy field for spirit contact, I accumulated everyone else's energy at the same time. All the people for whom I read, and anyone else in the studio audience, were tied to my energy field. By the time I got home to Los Angeles, I was sick with the flu. I felt as if I was carrying the weight of the world on my shoulders.

The best way to keep these bad energies away is to keep your energy healthy and upbeat. You have the power to say no to your own fearful and depressing thoughts. You also have the power to say no to other people. When you allow someone else to take charge of the way you think or what you are supposed to do, you give him or her the power to control you. Read on to find out how.

Your best offense is a strong defense.

Protect Yourself from Negative Thoughts and Emotions

Use this exercise to protect yourself from being drained of your energy. How do you know when to use this? If you feel more exhausted than usual, you may have encountered a person or situation that sucked the life out of you. That's when to use this.

Begin with your breathing meditation. Then imagine a cone of light dropping down on each side of you. The cones expand to engulf you completely. Concentrate on being completely sealed off so that nothing of a lower energy can penetrate your force field.

Now imagine the light pushing away any negative thoughts and energy. Imagine this shield of white light sending bad vibrations back to their source.

Keep visualizing the light surround you until you feel that the negativity has lifted and you feel centered.

Here's What Happens When You Have a Good Picture of Yourself

Brooke was a girl I met at one of my demonstrations. She had a pretty smile and was very easy to talk to. Her aura was filled with lots of blues and pinks, and I felt blessed to be in her presence.

At sixteen, she was confident and smart. She confided in me that she was still a virgin and never felt ashamed to admit it. "I want to get married and have a family one day, so if I am going to have sex, it has to be with someone who is mature and ready to commit to a relationship," she explained.

Brooke also lived under a lot of pressure. She had to work at a part-time job to help out with the family's finances, for instance. She did so gladly, however, because her parents gave her a lot of love and support.

Brooke had a great desire to understand other people and what they were going through, and that's what made her come to see me. "I figure if I can listen to others, I may learn something about myself," she said. She didn't need to judge anyone because she knew what it was like to be judged. "I had polio when I was a child, and still walk with a slight limp. When people find out, they usually feel sorry for me. But I can do everything anyone else can do."

Brooke was interested in going to college and majoring in anthropology. "I always wanted to learn different cultures and explore the unknown. I expect to be the same kind of person I am now when I grow up. I'm hoping work won't change me that much. At least I'll be someone my children will be proud of."

Brooke realized that having a good heart and balancing family, work, and school were more important than anything else she could do.

"You're a beautiful person on the inside as well as the outside," I said. "You have the opportunity to be a source of positive reinforcement for our planet. I see a lot of love in your aura. I think you will make a difference in a lot of people's lives."

SPIRIT SAYS . . .

You can fit in and still be yourself.
Making mistakes is part of the spiritual plan.
Don't give others the power to control you.
You can say no to fear and hate.
See yourself in a positive light.

Watch Out for Mind-Numbing Traps

You Have a Destiny to Fulfill

Dead or Alive!

You know how it feels when you're on a roller coaster and it's creeping up a steep hill. You know what's coming—the first big drop of the ride. You feel excited, scared, and exhilarated, all at the same time. Any moment, you're going to drop at a G-force intensity rate, and the thrill is on for the next two or three minutes. It's a mind-blowing ride from 0 to 3.2 G's in just seconds. And after it's over, you want to do it all over again because you feel so alive!

Now think of what life would be like without the thrill of such a ride. Numb! My question for you is: Why deaden yourself when you can be enjoying the roller coaster of life? That's what you do every time you fall into the mind-numbing traps of the ego. Here are some of its main warning signs.

Trap #1: Comparison

Have you ever said to yourself, "I have no talent"? Or, "I'm a nobody. I'll never do anything great"? Do you look around and always find someone else who is richer, smarter, cuter, and happier than you? Yeah, we all do.

Our society in general is built on the concepts of comparison and competition. If we don't outperform, outshine, out-something-or-other people around us, we're nobodies. Even criminals get more attention than we do. They do awful things, yet we parade them on TV shows because shock sells—or, should I say, *schlock* sells. What's wrong with this picture? Is it okay to do anything just to be noticed?

Comparison is the eternal runaround. You get to the top of the mountain, but instead of gazing at the glorious view, you look over to the next mountain peak. The one you're on is already a memory, and another is waiting to be conquered. That'll wear you down. You feel that you never quite make it, and whatever you do, it's never good enough. Comparing yourself to others crushes your creativity.

Every Christmastime, there's a classic movie called *It's a Wonderful Life* on TV. If you haven't seen it, catch it the next time around. It begins with the lead character, George Bailey, standing on a bridge ready to hurl himself into an icy river below. He thinks he is one giant failure. But Clarence, an angel-in-training, comes to his rescue. Clarence proceeds to show George what an impact he's made on others' lives and what his hometown, Bedford Falls, would have been like had George never been born at all. Scenes show George saving his brother from drowning, stopping the town pharmacist from accidentally poisoning someone, and helping poor people buy a home. The George-less Bedford Falls, meanwhile, is called Potterville, after Mr. Potter, a greedy old man, who winds up running the town, where everyone is pretty miserable. In the end, George realizes that he was not the big waste he thought he was. He realizes that his life, humble as it may have seemed, contributed greatly to the happiness and well-being of many people in Bedford Falls.

The movie was a flop when it came out in the 1940s, but over the years, it has become one of everyone's favorite feel-good movies. And as in the movie, we never really know about the timing of things or of the effect our lives have on any more than a handful of people. Yet the universe really does have a plan, and we are all a part of it. You and I have a definite and unique job to do, just like George Bailey did.

You are here to do what you are here to do, and your friend is here to do what he or she is here to do. There are no favorites, no winners, and no losers. Only the ego thinks in those terms. So do yourself a favor and stop comparing your life to someone else's. Your soul knows the lessons you have to learn. Besides, if you are comparing yourself to others, you'll have little energy left to do what is truly yours to do.

The universe is foolproof.

Trap #2: Expectations

Have you ever done something that you didn't want to do just to be cool or noticed, then lived to regret it? We all have. We all have lied, to ourselves or others, just to look good in someone else's eyes. The world is full of people who sacrifice their dreams to fulfill someone else's.

I almost did. My mom was a strong Irish-Catholic woman, and her wish was that one of her children would become a priest or a nun. I decided to be the one to make her wish come true, and enrolled in a seminary when I was fourteen. I thought this would make my mother so proud of me and love me all the more. I learned the hard way, though, that seminary life was no picnic. Most of the time I was lonely and depressed. I discovered that a lot of the other boys were as homesick as I was, too, adjusting to such an austere way of life. As a Catholic, I was caught in the "I must suffer" trap and figured that it was just what I had to do. For a while, it united me with all the other guys going through the same thing. I wanted to give my life to God, but found the seminary more like prison than a sanctuary.

I began to question God. Is God really what the priests say He is? Can I find God as a seminarian? My answer came on Good Friday when I sat in the chapel to pray.

As I stared at the gold chalice on the altar, I became aware of a peaceful presence filling the entire room. Then I had this feeling of calm and tranquility inside me. I knew that this feeling was really God; God just didn't hang out in a seminary or a church but was everywhere and in everyone. It was an incredible feeling of love.

After that Friday, I no longer felt obligated to stay in the seminary. Whatever I was there to learn I felt I had learned. I discovered a sense of self that I had never known before. I left the seminary after that first year, and in retrospect I am grateful for the experience. I realized that I could not live my mother's dream; I had to be true to myself.

Can Expectations Pressure You Too Much?

We all care what other people think of us or expect of us. I certainly wanted my mother to see me as special. We want to belong, to feel like part of a group. When we're young, this group is our family. When we get to junior high or middle school, this group becomes our friends, and we tend to gravitate to certain groups. If you're not in a clique, you're on the outs or a loner. If you're "in," you may have some anxiety that you'd better do what is expected. It's called peer pressure. You want to do what everyone else is doing, or out you go. It's hard to be true to yourself when you feel as though you must conform to some standard that is somebody else's idea.

Whether it's peer pressure or your own self-inflicted pressure to be liked or be cool or fit in, it boils down to the same thing: you're not being true to yourself.

When I returned to a New York City public high school after my year in the seminary, I met Jason, who was everyone's picture-perfect hero.

He was on both the football and basketball teams, and had several varsity letters. He was also pretty popular with the girls. Jason worked hard and spent a lot of time at practice. At the same time, his goal was to get into Harvard and one day become a doctor. But I never knew if that's what he wanted or what his father wanted.

Needless to say, Jason expected a lot from himself. I can remember when he got an A- on a history test and he turned red and stared out the window in disgust. Whoa! I thought. He IS hard on himself.

When everyone else was hanging out, Jason would be in the library or in the gym. I think he kept pushing himself because he wanted to please his dad. The family had high expectations for Jason to succeed.

Then, one day, there was some gossip going around the hallways saying that Jason had been caught shoplifting. I couldn't believe it. Not Jason! Not the football hero! Not the guy who wanted to get into Harvard. Why would anyone start such a rumor?

The next day, I learned that it was true. Jason had spent the night in jail. I knew he must have been totally humiliated when his dad came to bail him out.

Jason returned to school but kept to himself. He dropped out of football and basketball. I wanted to ask him what had happened, but I couldn't bring myself to do it. So I was surprised when he came up to me one day.

"I guess I just couldn't please everyone," he said. "I know I wasn't having a good time. I guess getting into trouble was the only way I knew to get everyone off my back."

"Couldn't you just tell them?" I asked.

"I couldn't face their disappointment."

"But you did anyway."

"I guess I did. But somehow I feel relieved. Now I can just be myself."

Jason demanded perfection of himself as he strove to please others. Instead of just expressing his true feelings, he lied to himself and everyone else. In the end, no one was satisfied.

Signpost #7: You can only please yourself.

What are some of the expectations you have of yourself?

_____

_____

Are they realistic?

_____

_____

What expectations do you have of others?

_____

_____

Are your expectations of others realistic or some form of control?

_____

_____

Trap #3: Fear

Love bonds people and fear separates them. When we come to earth, we bring our karmic obligations and past-life experiences with us. But our personality is a blank slate, and we develop a fresh new identity in each and every lifetime. This is what makes each life so unique.

As we grow up, we are shaped by our parents' beliefs and the judgments of our teachers, friends, and classmates. We are drawn into the trap of the world's lower nature, which revolves around fear. When we persist in thoughts of fear, we create a powerful energy force that becomes our reality.

Show Me the Money!

One of the most consistent fears in this world is that of not having enough money. And the more one persists in this thought, the less money one seems to have. Yet the world is an abundant place. Everything you need and want is available.

Jeff and Tim's father left them when they were very young, and their mother had a tough time finding a job that would pay all the bills. They lost their house and had to move in to a small apartment. Things were pretty tight, and on their meager budget, luxuries became a thing of the past.

When their mother decided to go back to college and get a degree in teaching, Jeff and Tim started to worry that they would become homeless. "We won't have enough money to live on," they told her. "You can't just go back to school. What about us?"

Their mother, however, was determined to finally live the dream she'd had since she was a little girl. She found a way to get a grant and was able to attend school and work part-time. Even so, there were times when she had to go on welfare to make ends meet. If things got really bad, she would quit school for a semester to earn more money.

It was an uncomfortable situation for Jeff and Tim. They were thoroughly embarrassed when the holidays rolled around and everyone at school displayed the presents they'd received. All Jeff and Tim got was a turkey basket from the church.

After six years, their mother got her degree and was ready to teach. Meanwhile, Jeff and Tim were in high school and had jobs at Kmart to help out. When Jeff was a junior, he applied for a scholarship at the University of California in Berkeley.

Both Jeff and Tim graduated from college. Jeff now has a great job in a bank, and Tim has followed his mother's example and become a teacher. It's clear that money, or the lack of it, didn't stop them from accomplishing their goals. Yes, sometimes it was scary to be living on the edge, and Jeff and Tim did without a lot of the extras their peers had, but they always had what they needed. They had each other's love as soulmates, learning a very difficult lesson.

If Jeff, Tim, and their mother had spent all their time moaning about their fate, afraid to go out the door, and focusing on what they didn't have, they probably would not have made it too far. Hardship is what you make of it. You don't have to let fear get the best of you.

> ## It's always darkest before the dawn, but the dawn always comes!

HOW TO CONTROL YOUR FEAR

- Start replacing the negative with the positive. Practice this mantra: "Healthy am I, happy am I, holy am I."
- If you want good in your life, do good in your life. You cannot expect happiness if you make everyone else's life miserable.
- Do your breathing meditation and ask for guidance from Spirit.

Trap #4: Guilt

Guilt, expectation, and fear are like the three musketeers. They hang out with one another to play a twisted mind game.

When Sara, a beautiful sixteen-year-old came to see me, I could tell she was in terrible distress. I wondered why, at such a young age, she was coming in at all, but then it wasn't up to me to judge. I started the reading, and immediately another teen appeared. She looked exactly like the one sitting in front of me.

"This is weird," I said. "I am seeing double. I feel like you two are almost the same."

"She is my twin, Samantha," Sara answered.

"Twins! No wonder."

Sara smiled.

"Your sister is around you a lot. Have you felt her?"

"She comes to me in my dreams, if that's what you mean."

"Yes, dreams are a way in which a spirit will communicate."

"She is saying people couldn't tell you apart. She is laughing about how they would mix you two up."

Sara just sat there quietly.

Suddenly, I was overcome with emotion. "Your sister says it was time for her to go. She loves you very much."

Sara broke down and started to sob uncontrollably. "It's all my fault she died. I'm so sorry. Please tell her I'm sorry."

I could feel the love coming from Samantha, and feel the pain coming from her twin.

"Sara, your sister wants me to tell you that it was not your fault that she died. It was her time. You have to stop feeling guilty. Do you know the name Matt?" I asked.

Sara looked horrified at the mention of this name.

"She wants you to know that Matt is okay. Please don't hate yourself. You were not to blame."

Although I didn't understand what was going on, I hoped that it all made sense to Sara.

I spoke softly to her. "Your sister loves you very much."

Sara cried for a few moments. Then she picked her head up and began to unravel the mystery of her sister's communication.

"Samantha was always the good one. I was always going out with the wild kids. I hated school and she loved it. One day, Matt came to our house on his motorcycle. I wasn't home, but Samantha was. He could never tell us apart. I guess Samantha thought it would be fun to play me, so she went off on the bike with Matt. Only . . ." Sara broke down again. "Only, they had an accident. Some truck pulled out and cut in front of them. Their bike slid under the truck and they were crushed under the wheels."

Sara dropped her head and tears just flowed. "It was all my fault. If I didn't hang out with Matt and the other kids, this wouldn't have happened. My sister would still be alive today. If God wanted to punish me for being bad, why didn't I die instead of her?"

I was very touched by this young woman and her overwhelming feelings of guilt.

"God doesn't punish us," I said tenderly. "We punish ourselves."

I tried to reassure Sara that the soul never dies, and her sister was not in any physical pain when she passed over. No one was to blame. "Your sister's karmic obligations were over, and she went back home."

After a while, Sara wiped away her tears. "I am glad that I came here. I felt so responsible for Samantha's death."

"Your sister loves you and will be watching over you," I told her.

Sara left my office feeling lighter. Her self-condemnation was over.

Guilt is created by our own self-imposed expectations and fears. Our mind runs the guilt trip over and over. There is no advantage to feeling guilty. Guilt just clouds our ability to see things as they really are.

It's hard to face someone else when you can't face yourself.

Trap #5: Dishonesty

It's hard to change our circumstances if we spend our energy hiding our true feelings. A lot of people do it, I know. No one wants to come clean. You say things you really don't mean because you don't want to hurt someone else's feelings. But then you do hurt someone's feelings—your own. You lie about something because you're afraid of the consequences. But the fear that comes from hiding the deception can be just as scary.

Haven't you noticed that when you pretend to like something or somebody, you quickly start feeling bad inside? You feel trapped into doing something that you really don't want to do?

Dishonesty is a form of denial. If you're in denial, you can't fix the problem, you only make it worse.

Gary started taking money out of his mother's purse to play poker with his friends. For a while, he was getting away with it, and it seemed easier every time he did it. Then one day his mother confronted him.

"Gary, I seem to be missing some money from my purse. Do you know anything about it?"

"Who, me?" Gary said with a shocked expression. "No, Mom, I don't know. Maybe you spent it and forgot."

The next time Gary took money, his mother confronted him again.

"Gary, I've been counting my money every day, and I know I'm missing twenty dollars. Did you take it?"

"Mom, I swear I'm not taking your money."

The next time Gary stole money from his mother, his father came up to his room.

"Gary, your mother tells me that you're stealing money from her purse. What's going on?"

"Dad, I swear I'm not taking her money. She must be spending it herself."

"Why would your mother blame you for something she's doing?"

"I don't know," Gary said awkwardly.

At this point, Gary was so caught up in his lying that he couldn't tell the truth. Meanwhile, his poker debts mounted up, and his need for more money escalated. He not only took money from his mother's purse but his sister's wallet as well. His sister caught him in the act and stopped him.

Now that he was discovered, Gary had to come clean.

Gary's parents angrily declared, "You're grounded for a month! It's bad enough that you stole money, but then you kept doing it and lying about it over and over again."

"I needed the money," Gary explained. "Besides, I thought if I could get away with it, why not?"

"I'm sorry, son. You've let your mother and me down," his father said. "I don't know if we can trust you in the future."

Gary's dishonesty not only caused unhappiness for his family, but was also a blow to his own self-worth. To be a trustworthy person takes work and staying power, but it takes only one incident to tear it all down.

Eventually, all your lies catch up with you. When you are found out, you often feel worse than you would have if you had told the truth in the first place. Why feel like a slug? You don't want to kill your chances of being seen as someone who can handle things. Whatever the problem, it's not going to disappear by closing your eyes, wishing it away, or lying about it.

The truth will set you free.

Name five things you lie about.

1. _____

2. _____

3. _____

4. _____

5. _____

Now, see if there is one thing you can do differently to be more honest about each of these five things.

1. _____

2. _____

3. _____

4. _____

5. _____

James Van Praagh

Stop Whining . . .
and Do Something

Be Responsible for Yourself

The Perfect Daughter

Brenda came to me after one of my demonstrations. She was fifteen. I could tell she was feeling down just by the expression on her face.

"My mother is a teacher and she wants me to be a teacher like her. I do everything I am told; I'm a pretty good daughter. But, Mr. Van Praagh, I don't want to be a teacher."

"Have you told your mother this?" I asked.

"Well, yes and no. Not exactly. It's hard to talk to her."

"What do you mean?" I pressed her.

"She always calls me stupid. She's very smart. Every time I'm around her, I always act dumb in front of her. I don't know why. I'm a lot better with my friends. But with her, I just can't seem to get things right."

"I'm beginning to understand. Maybe your mom intimidates you. You try to be the perfect daughter that she wants you to be, but you can't live up to her standards. Am I headed in the right direction?" I asked.

My heart went out to this young woman who felt beaten down and discouraged.

"It's never good enough for Mom," Brenda said, her lips quivering and tears starting to drip down her cheeks.

"Well, let's see if I can help with that," I responded. "I want you to start a journal, so you can start writing down your feelings about your mother and yourself. If you can't talk to your mom, I want you to write her little notes and tell her how you feel when she calls you stupid. You don't have to give her these notes, but you can if you feel like it will help you. Can you do that?"

"Yes, that sounds easy, as long as I don't have to give her the notes," Brenda agreed. "I don't want her to yell at me and put me down."

"Whatever you want. Then I want you to use your imagination and see how you would like your mother to act toward you. See her praising you and saying all these good things about you. Write all this down in your journal so you can remember to do this little visualization every day. Do you think you can do that?"

I could see the energy around Brenda brighten. At that moment, she felt a little less powerless.

"Let me know how you are doing," I said.

REALITY CHECK

Believe it or not, no one can make you do something if you really don't want to, not even your parents. That's right—not even them. You always have a choice, even though it may not appear that way. By this I mean that you can either follow their rules while you're living with them, or you can leave. Most of you are not ready to leave, so you follow the rules whether you like them or not. So, you really are making a choice, whether you see it that way or not.

"I definitely will," she said, waving good-bye.

When I heard from Brenda again, she told me that her relationship with her mother was slowly but surely improving.

When you blame someone else for your life not working, like Brenda was doing, you actually see the world upside down. Blame causes uncertainty and limitation, and you actually push away the thing that you want. You definitely feel powerless. When you take responsibility for yourself, you create an energy force that says "I accept." It's sort of like holding your arms open wide. You are in charge because you create the space for the thing you want to come to you.

Signpost #8: To change your situation, change your attitude.

Anyone Can Turn Lemons into Lemonade

A few years ago, I attended a benefit for an environmental organization. As I reached for a spinach puff at the buffet table, another hand grabbed for the same thing. I looked up and saw a familiar face.

"Marky!" I exclaimed in surprise.

Mark looked a little more mature since I had seen him several years earlier, when he was seventeen. I'd originally met him as a client. He had come to me on the advice of a counselor who hoped that Mark might be able to resolve past conflicts with his mother if he had the opportunity to contact her in spirit.

Mark had endured a difficult childhood. His brother was killed right before his eyes; his father was an alcoholic and his mother a drug user. He was shuffled from one foster home to another, and never got a true sense of what it meant to be part of a family.

When he reached ninth grade, Mark could no longer take the bullying and crude comments from the insensitive kids at school, so he dropped out. He moved into a small one-room apartment and began working in a video store.

Now here we were, meeting by chance a few years down the road.

We sat down together and Mark told me what had happened since we'd last been in touch.

"I quit the video store," Mark told me. "They accused me of stealing, which I hadn't. Without a job, I couldn't pay the rent, so I wound up on the street, homeless. That was the beginning of my descent into hell."

Like his mother, Mark entered a world of drugs. "I was so hooked on crack, I couldn't tell which end was up."

"How did you get out of it?" I asked.

Mark stuttered and then said, "I found God—"

Uh-oh, I immediately thought, he's going to start preaching.

"—inside of me," he finished, interrupting my thoughts.

"I was literally lying on the curb staring at this billboard of Tom Hanks in some movie. I remember thinking, 'This guy is nobody special, just a guy who made a movie. What's so different between him and me? I'm not a loser. I can be somebody that everyone respects, too!' As soon as that thought crossed my mind, a car backed over my foot. A woman got out. She looked at me and was very upset. I was so out of it, but she managed to get me to the hospital."

I just sat there listening to Mark in amazement.

"She was an angel sent by God. While I was in the hospital, I went through detox. I also did a lot of soul searching. I realized that there was no one to blame but me if my life was screwed up. I had to take responsibility for the future and knew I needed some support to make things change. Isn't that what we're all here to learn?"

I could not believe this was the same kid I had met eight years ago.

"The woman who ran me over helped me to believe in myself. I mattered to her. She said she could see the light in my eyes. She introduced me to a friend who owned a glass company. I began to work for him and learned about the business. Then I had an idea about etching color designs onto the glass. That was the beginning. He let me create my own glass pieces and sell them. Now I am selling them all over the world."

"That's incredible," I said.

Mark was a teen who had faced many obstacles in life. You might think that a person in his circumstances didn't have much of a chance. But he looked at himself and decided to do something about his situation. With perseverance, determination, and belief in himself, Mark managed to change a road to nowhere to a road to somewhere, and he found a more meaningful life.

Don't get stuck in reverse.

Take Charge of Your Destiny

Most of the time, we let life happen to us instead of taking charge and choosing the life we want to live. But like Mark, we can choose to be in charge of our destiny. He could have stayed in the gutter and died from

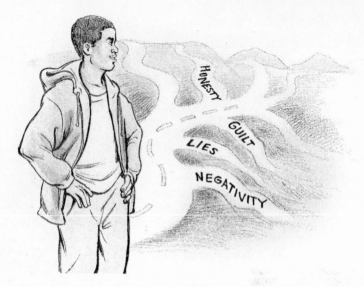

an overdose of drugs. Instead, he seized an opportunity and created a better life for himself.

It's important to remember here that with choice comes responsibility. That's not a bad thing. Think of responsibility as something good instead of something that should be avoided. Interchange the word *responsibility* for *freedom*. Without one we cannot have the other. I know it's a lot easier to slack off and not take responsibility for our problems. We would rather indulge in an attitude that says life sucks and we can't do a thing about it, but this attitude leaves us with very few options to create something worthwhile.

It's also easier to point the finger and blame someone else for your mistakes. Blaming others is another way of saying that you're not in charge. You turn yourself into a victim. Being a victim implies that you have no choice and no responsibility. No one expects much from a victim.

It takes responsibility to step up to the plate and hit a home run. After all, everyone is watching. There is a lot of pressure. It's much easier to stay in the dugout and not risk striking out. But if you do hit a home run, there is no greater feeling of accomplishment. If you don't, no one can blame you for not trying.

Being responsible for your choices is part of your spiritual growth. Willingness to learn and take responsibility is part of your karmic makeup. So, take a good look at where you are in your life. You got here by the choices you have made thus far. The choice to change is always yours. You decide.

James Van Praagh

List some of the choices you have made that you would change if you could.

_____

_____

_____

_____

_____

Drugs and Alcohol: The Black Hole of Choices

Too often have I seen the devastation a child's death causes parents. But it's not just parents: the loss of one so young also has a disturbing effect on the child's brothers, sisters, aunts, uncles, teachers, and friends. Many times these tragedies are caused by teens driving drunk or under the influence of drugs.

A mother once saw me on the TV show *The Other Side* and contacted me for a reading. Her son had been killed driving home after a day out with his friends at Magic Mountain, celebrating their high school graduation.

The whole family attended the meeting at my house. They were very anxious to get in touch with the spirit world to know that everything was all right with him.

"Your son is here. I can tell he is a practical joker."

"Yes, that's Chris."

"Chris has come with some friends of his. Who is Jonathan or John? He is about nineteen years old. He passed from a drug overdose. You don't know him, but you will meet his parents."

The mother nodded as if to say okay.

"Did Chris slam into something?" I asked.

"Yes," said his mother.

"Was it a tree?"

"Yes."

"I feel your son went unconscious right away. I feel that he was at fault. This situation has taught him about responsibility. It taught him about the preciousness of life."

His mother answered. "I knew Chris would have a few beers at his friend's house. It was probably a mixture of alcohol and fatigue that caused him to fall asleep at the wheel."

"He is saying he was very lucky to have you as parents because of your understanding of him. He says that love is letting the person be who he is, on his own path, and being willing to let him grow. He wants you to know that he continues to grow on the other side. I feel there was trouble with him. He was always looking for adventure and excitement. You had to lay down rules for him early on. Do you understand?"

"Yes, that's right."

"He is saying, 'I'm sorry for causing you a lot of trouble and grief.' He wants to tell you he is learning about love over there. He loves you guys very much, and loves you for coming here. He thanks you."

Chris's mother felt a lot of guilt about her son's death. So did his father, brother, and sister. They all had unfinished business with Chris. They were filled with many different emotions, including sadness, hurt, and even joy. They were also angry that Chris left too soon with so much life ahead of him. Like many others who lose a daughter or son to alcohol or drug abuse, everyone in a family experiences a certain amount of turmoil over the often-irresponsible behavior of another member.

You may think that drinking and drugging only affects you, but it doesn't. Remember, you and everyone else in your life are all part of a soul group. When one member of the group is involved, the other members are also affected.

The worst thing about drinking and using drugs is that they deplete your energy. This makes you vulnerable to the negative influences of other people, and you get caught up in a cycle of attracting the very thing that hurts you.

I know it can be very hard to say no to your friends when they ask you to drink or do drugs. For the moment, you may feel stuck for a way out of something you really don't want to do. What will they think of me? keeps running through your mind. This is a true test of your sense of who you are. The drinking and drugging won't make them like you any better. It doesn't work that way. If they are really your friends, they'll love you the way you are.

Ask yourself: What am I trying to find out if I take these drugs? If you are trying to feel free or less stressed out or are doing it to show your independence from your parents, think of other ways to do the same thing. If you're cool with asking your parents about drugs, then talk to them. They had to deal with drugs and drinking when they were teens.

Remember, your parents are your soulmates!

If a friend asks you to go drinking or to take drugs, think of three things you could do instead. For instance, you could go to a movie, take your dog for a walk, visit the mall, skateboard, ride your bike, buy a CD, dance, surf, play basketball, or any number of other things. List something that you love to do either by yourself or with a group. The only requirement is that it has to make you feel good about yourself.

_____

_____

_____

So Many Choices, So Little Time

You're with your friend at the mall. She walks into a store and you see her shoplifting a CD off the rack. You're shocked and upset. What do you do? Do you confront her and tell her she's wrong, and risk losing her friendship? Or do you stay silent and in essence con-

done her bad behavior? Choices like this one can be difficult. Doing the right thing is not as easy as it sounds. Our ego and emotions cloud our decisions. Ultimately, we have to live with the choices we make.

THAT'S NOT COOL! I WON'T BE AROUND YOU IF YOU STEAL.

There is another way. You can make a spiritual choice—one that takes into account the physical, emotional, and spiritual consequences. A spiritual choice is not made by your ego or out of fear, nor does it accumulate karmic debt. A spiritual choice is a responsible choice.

When you allow your true self to help you choose, you are aware of how your actions will affect others. This doesn't mean that you become a people pleaser or sacrifice your needs for another's. Being true to yourself means you're true to everyone else. Choosing from a higher perspective takes the struggle out of a situation and helps you to find a solution that is best for everyone involved, including you.

Three years ago, I had to say good-bye to a friend because she was doing something that was hurtful to other friends of mine. I could see dark clouds of energy around her, and I didn't want that kind of energy around me. For self-preservation, I had to make the cut. Some time after that, I ran into her in a store. Her energy had cleared up, and I could feel that she was in a good space once again. It wasn't hard picking up where we left off.

James Van Praagh

Sometimes the hardest choice to make is the one that might hurt someone else. Ending a relationship or telling your friend that something he or she did was wrong are choices that might cause immediate discomfort. In the long run, however, such a choice may turn out to be a great liberating force. Your decision may urge your friend to reexamine her attitude or change his pattern of self-destruction, and you meanwhile will have the comfort of knowing that you made a wise decision. Your friends are part of your soul group, and when you speak the truth, you are helping your soulmate no matter which decision he or she makes.

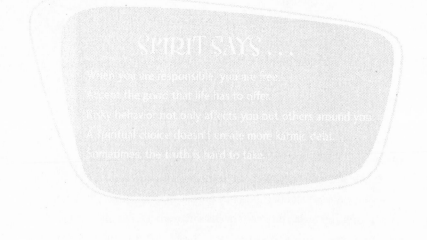

SPIRIT SAYS . . .

When you are responsible, you are free.
Accept the good that life has to offer.
Risky behavior not only affects you but others around you.
A spiritual choice doesn't create more karmic debt.
Sometimes the truth is hard to take.

The Genius Inside You Is Trying to Get Out

Use Your Creative Energy

Open Sesame

Creativity is the ability to turn ideas, feelings, and expressions into physical form. Everyone, not only artists, musicians, writers, and actors, is creative. Each person has creative energy and can use this energy to accomplish anything, especially making life easier.

When you use your creativity, your soul is a happy camper. You are expressing your uniqueness—what makes you you.

Look at the world and all of creation. Pretty amazing how so many things have been created from a single thought or idea, isn't it? But that's how creativity works. You have a thought, and you take that thought and build upon it. It's a step-by-step process. You may even get others to help you with your idea, and their ideas contribute to your original thought.

Everyone can up their creativity quotient. Here's how you can do it:

- Nurture your self-esteem. Learn who you are and love who you are.
- Validate your intuition and instincts. Don't look outside yourself for all the answers.
- Hang out with people who are positive and happy. If your parents are negative, find a teacher, coach, or friend who has a more cheerful attitude and learn from them.
- When you do something good, and you are praised, don't say, "Oh, it was nothing." Say thank you and recognize your accomplishment.
- Be aware of your dreams— the ones that come when you sleep.

Signpost #9: You were born to be creative.

Write some of the things you would like to do but are afraid to do because you might look foolish.

_____

_____

_____

Keep this list and look at it every day. Before long, you may start to feel inspired to do one or more of the things on it.

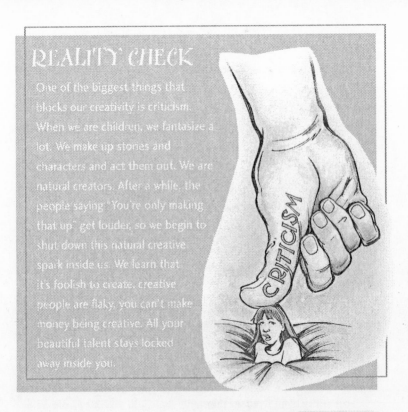

Creativity is the spark of life.

You Can Run, But You Can't Hide

Carrie was a creative kid. She liked to find old junk and make it into something else. She would explore her neighborhood in search of discarded tables, chairs, or lamps that she could make over into something brand new. At fifteen, Carrie had made a lot of trash into treasures and would sell her artistic achievements at yard sales. The only problem was that Carrie was not a people person. She didn't have a good sense of her own identity outside of her art and was very sensitive to what people said and did.

Carrie became infatuated with Ryan, who was part of a fast crowd at school. She didn't know how to deal with these kids, so she just went along. Ryan took her to some late-night parties where drugs flowed freely. Carrie began using Ecstasy. She was swept up in the excitement of having friends around her. It was all so new to her.

Then, at one rave party, Carrie saw a girl lose consciousness and fall to the floor. Someone called 911, and most of the kids evacuated the place. When the ambulance arrived, the paramedics were able to resuscitate the girl who had overdosed. They quickly rushed her to the hospital.

At that moment, Carrie thought, What am I doing to myself? This is not who I am. Why am I here?

The next day at school, Carrie found out that the girl from the party survived, thank goodness. When Ryan came to her locker and asked her to another party, she looked at him and said, "Aren't you upset about last night? That could have been you or me on the floor."

Ryan looked at Carrie and said, "No way. I know what I'm doing."

Carrie really liked Ryan and thought she could save him from a life of partying and drugs. She decided to go with him and make sure he

REALITY CHECK

Too much TV can actually numb your creative juices. Francis Ford Coppola, the Academy Award–winning director and cowriter of *The Godfather*, once said in a magazine article that if he wanted to come up with something original, he would have to give up TV for a year. It's hard to be creative when your mind is turning to mush.

wouldn't get too loaded. At the party, Carrie felt like an outsider. She realized that these kids were not interested in being friends, but were running away from something. She looked at Ryan and felt she couldn't help him unless he really wanted to help himself. But he was already getting high.

"I'm leaving," Carrie told Ryan. Ryan just smiled and waved good-bye.

That week, Carrie learned that she did know something about herself—she could stand up for herself. She resumed her trash-to-treasure artwork and began to feel good about herself. By expressing her creativity, Carrie was being more herself than any drug could make her feel.

Like Carrie, we are all in need of some form of creative recovery. When you express yourself, no matter what form that may take, you will find that life becomes more rewarding, and you are being true to the real you.

Creativity is not passive.

What an Inspiring Idea!

You always hear artists or writers say, "I have to be inspired," "I'm waiting for my juices to flow," or something like that. What is inspiration, anyway? The word simply means "a divine influence on a person." The invisible spiritual forces are always around us, and one of the ways a spirit communicates is through inspirational thought. You might think of this as spirits superimposing their thoughts on ours, much like superimposing one picture over another one.

A good way to make yourself open to inspiration is to rest your mind. Relaxation, in whatever form it takes, helps us to get into the right frame of mind to accept inspiration. Relaxation doesn't always mean lying down—there are many ways people relax. Still, relaxation is necessary: I find that when you don't struggle for it, inspiration comes much more easily.

Meditation and quieting the mind are some of the ways to open the channel to the spiritual forces, making it easy for inspiration to come through. Writing in your journal is another way to help get the creative juices going. Expressing your thoughts in written form also helps you to release pent-up emotions like sadness, anger, and frustration, clearing your mind for more creative ideas.

Open Up to Inspirational Thought

Try this exercise in bed before going to sleep at night. You can listen to the radio or a CD, but keep the music in the background. Let your mind relax. Take at least three deep breaths. Following the rhythm of your breath, relax your body to where you are feeling calm and almost ready for sleep. As you keep breathing, let thoughts just pass through. Try not to hold on to them; let them pop in, but keep them moving. When you are ready, you can open your eyes and jot down your thoughts in your journal.

Dreaming Up a New Idea

We've all heard someone explain something away as "only a dream." However, dreams are much more important than most people realize. Dreams are communication from your unconscious mind, a vast source of creativity, and your connection to the cosmic forces. If you have a problem to solve, sleep on it. The answer is inside waiting to surface when your waking mind goes to sleep. This is the time when your soul takes inventory of what you have been doing and gives you practical guidance. This is also a time when your spirit guides communicate to you. Why can't this happen when you're awake? Usually, your waking mind is so packed with the day's activity, worry, and judgment, that sometimes the

REALITY CHECK

How can dreams help your creativity? Let's take a look at some creators. On an A&E television series about writers, I once saw a segment about Robert Louis Stevenson, the author of several classics, including *Treasure Island* and *The Strange Case of Dr. Jekyll and Mr. Hyde*. Interestingly enough, he got most of the ideas for his books from his dreams. As soon as he woke up in the morning, he would sit at his desk and write down his dreams word for word. These dreams eventually became his novels. Imagine waking up in that house! Stevenson wasn't the only famous personality to use his dreams in his line of work. Inventor Thomas A. Edison, the composer Wolfgang Amadeus Mozart, and even Albert Einstein have all been given prolific ideas in dreams.

obvious is not obvious enough. Your mind is at work 24/7, and some of its best work is done in your dreams.

What Are the Alligators Doing in My Dreams?

Actually, dreams are pretty cool, if you can get past the weirdness of their symbols. Think of them as mystery movies. Everything means something, but what? If I dream that my teeth are falling out, will they? Not likely. Teeth are symbolic, and the symbols are different for everyone. What do teeth represent to you? Teeth may have a whole other meaning for your friend. You get to figure symbols out based on your life. And, if you want to find out more about dreams, there are a ton of books on how to interpret them.

Besides giving you creative insight, dreams can certainly help you to understand your feelings. Having dreams in which you are being chased or attacked? Look at your present circumstances. Don't take it as an omen, because dreams only refer to the present unless you have a recurring dream. When you have a recurring dream—a dream that you dream every week or every month or just a few times in a few years—you are being bothered by something from your past that has yet to be resolved. Most people have recurring dreams for a certain period of time, and then the dream stops. That stoppage means that the issue has been somehow settled.

Mostly, your dreams are about something that is happening to you right now. Perhaps it is a sticky situation you cannot figure out. Someone or something may be bothering you. What you feel in the dream is probably what you feel when you're awake, only you may not be paying attention while awake. If you have stress going on in your life, and you're not taking care of it, your dreams will re-create it in a very dramatic way as you sleep. When you change the situation, you'll stop getting those nightmares.

The presence of people in your dreams is another way that your dreams use dramatic license. Dreams are about you, even if you dream about Tommy, Mary, or Jack. The dream uses people you are familiar with to show you something about yourself. You not only star in your dream, but you get to play all the parts, too. Ask yourself: What about so-and-so reminds me of me?

And if you dream about a movie star (who doesn't?), it probably is an angel or spirit guide coming to you in disguise.

> You don't have to be a rocket scientist to understand your dreams.

Remembering Your Dreams

To get the most information and ideas from your dreams, it would help to remember them. How else can you come up with some great story like Robert Louis Stevenson or unique creation like Thomas Edison? If nothing else, your dream will make a great icebreaker at the next party you attend.

The easiest way to remember a dream is by talking about it. When you talk about your dreams, you send a message to your subconscious mind that you are serious about remembering them.

Keep a pocket tape recorder or a journal by your bed—you may even want to use your computer if that is close by. As soon as you wake up, record your first impressions, capture the feelings and pictures from your dreams. The more you write down or record your dreams, the more you will remember.

SPIRIT SAYS . . .

Everyone is creative.

Creativity takes ideas and makes them real.

It's okay to look foolish.

Be original. Turn off the TV.

Spirits inspire us through our thoughts.

Dreams can help you understand yourself.

The Energy of the Universe Is Always in Motion

Your Wishes Can Come True

Are You Prepared to Succeed?

Amber was a freshman at an all-girls high school. Being new to the area, she knew no one. She was uptight being around the other girls, most of whom knew one another. In class, she kept to herself and stayed in the back of the room like a quiet little mouse. If you had to size Amber up, you would think she was either a loner or had something to hide.

Deep down, though, Amber was just unbearably shy. She wanted to meet the other girls at school, but she didn't know how to make the first move. Finally, Amber thought to herself, If I am ever going to meet anyone, I will have to do something about it.

Once that thought came to mind, the universe responded. One day, Amber noticed a girl walking around the classroom giving out papers. She did this every day. She also spent time talking and fooling around with some of the girls. I can do that, Amber thought. So, in her sophomore year, Amber volunteered to pass around the daily papers in homeroom. At first, she just smiled at each girl, but then she began to talk and get to know each one. Eventually, she even joked around with them. Amber was on her way to making some friends and enjoying high school more each day.

But Amber didn't stop there: she decided to try out for the drama group. It was hard breaking in, as the drama coach had her favorites. How can I be like them? Amber wondered. By being in a play, of course! Yet all the seniors got the real parts—sophomores got the leftovers.

Amber knew that she had to show she could act if she ever hoped to be considered for a role in the spring play. So she went to the library and found a one-act play to showcase her talents. She formed a group of other sophomore players, and they rehearsed by themselves. Then they presented the play to the drama coach.

At the next sophomore assembly, Amber and her cast were asked to put on their play. They were an instant hit. The teachers persuaded the coach to present the play at both the junior and senior class assemblies. By then, too, many of the students at school recognized Amber, and gave her thumbs-up or high fives.

When auditions came around for the spring play, Amber got one of the principal leads. She was becoming a very popular kid at school.

By junior year, Amber was involved in math club, honor society, and, of course, drama club. In her senior year, Amber was voted senior class president.

So how did one utterly shy girl become the most popular kid at school?

From one thought, Amber took action. It's amazing that when an intention is honest and real, and you take one step toward your dream, the universe responds to you.

AT LEAST I WON'T BE REJECTED.

Whatever you can do or dream, begin it now.

Pick Your Priorities

Every thought you have, especially ones with emotional feelings behind them, creates a force of energy. Most of the time, we let these thoughts flit in and out of our heads without doing much about them. The energy for the thought soon disappears, and what could have been recedes into the sea of thoughts.

Often people tell me that they have some idea that they don't pursue. Then, about a month or six months later, they see their idea on some TV program. Thoughts are all around us, and if you don't do something with the ones that come to you, someone else will.

With all the thoughts rumbling around in your mind, you have to decide which ones are important to you. Like Amber, you have to prioritize what it is you really want. Here are some of the things that teens tell me are high priorities:

- **Getting a driver's license**
- **Going from being a C student to an A student**
- **Getting into college**
- **Making an athletic team**
- **Getting a part-time job**
- **Having a date for the prom or the homecoming dance**
- **Getting enough sleep**

In order to achieve these goals, you will have to schedule your time to prioritize your responsibilities from week to week. Making a simple plan doesn't have to be difficult. Take fifteen minutes a week to list the things you want to accomplish. You may find that you will be completing more than you thought. For instance, if you want to raise your average in school from a C to an A, here are some things you might put on your list:

1. Finish homework every night.

2. Go over some of the tests you got back from the teacher to see where your mistakes are.

3. Add a half hour to your daily study time.

Pick a priority for next week, and list some actions you can do to achieve it:

_____

_____

_____

_____

Signpost #10:
The universe rewards action!

If You Can Dream It, You Can Do It

Everything in the world is created from a thought. When your mind joins with the mind of the universe, something is created. Do you want to learn how to tap into this giant universal mind and get what you want?

The first thing to remember is that like attracts like. If you want A, you can't be thinking of B. If you want to get a date, you can't think that you're a loser and that nobody likes you, and expect to get a date. It just doesn't work like that. When you have decided on something you really want, there are four steps you can take toward attaining it:

1. Define your intention. Why do you want that date? Is it to inflate your ego? Do you want to help someone? Do you want to feel better about yourself? Do you want to be more sociable? There has to be a reason to want something. If there isn't, chances are you'll move on to something else.

2. Be specific about what you want, the more specific the better. Fill in the details. "I want to take my date to the Halloween party. I'll be going as The Rock."

3. Believe that you can have what you want, and that you deserve it. Remember, we all have beliefs. If you say it, but don't believe it possible, it's as if you're driving a car with your foot on the brake. You can't get very far like that.

4. Live the goal as if it has already happened—as if you have what you want right now. See yourself with your date having a good time.

REALITY CHECK

Define your intention! What is your reason for wanting something? Pure intention does not include judgment or ego, like wanting to be rich and famous just to be rich and famous. Pure intention comes from your heart. It has strength of purpose. If you want to be a singer, for instance, your intention is to sing, not to be a millionaire. If your intention as a singer is to work hard and be the best you can be, then perhaps a by-product of your hard work could be millions of dollars. Whenever you have more than one intention about the same thing, you become conflicted, and usually the purest intention wins out. When you think with your ego instead of your heart, you begin to doubt that you'll get what you want. Your ego says, "You've never had that before, what makes you think you can have it now?" Lack and limitation enter the energy field of what you are trying to achieve. Put your heart into the process, not your big fat head.

Some Things Are Too Big for Willpower Alone

Many people think that if you want something, you can get it through sheer willpower. Yes, willpower *will* get you what you want for the short term, but it's very hard to keep it going. If you are trying to use your willpower, say, to give up junk food, or stop biting your nails, or be on time, you will find that you can will yourself to do it for perhaps a week or two. After that, you'll be back to the same routine of snacking on junk food every chance you get or biting your nails or being late. Willpower can help get you started, but pure intention will sustain the long haul.

As a spiritual being, everything you need is within you. You don't have to stress and strain to make things happen. That is part of the erroneous thinking of the world in which we live. You do have to think of what you want and take a step toward it. Even if you don't know how to do it all, it's amazing how one step leads to the next. Remember that you're an energy being and energy is always in motion.

Let Go of Preconceived Ideas

Thoughts and ideas are always flowing through you, but you can block that flow of energy when you try to control a situation. When you try to control how a thing is supposed to happen, you're afraid the universe won't understand you or will mix you up with the kid down the street. You don't trust things to turn out right. However, the universe understands what you want. If you order a cheeseburger, the universe knows the difference between cheeseburgers and tacos, so it doesn't bring you a plate of tacos. If you try to control the process or the outcome, you will miss all the opportunities that the universe sends your way. You have to be open to new and different ways—ways you may have not even thought of.

I once heard a story about a man drowning at sea. He looked up to

Faith is believing in things when common sense tells you not to.

heaven and said, "Please God, help me." In a few seconds, a log came floating by, but the man didn't think it was sturdy enough. So, he kept praying. "Please, God, help me." As he splashed around in panic, he missed a boat that sailed by. By now, he was going down for the third time, and, with his last breath pleaded, "Please, God, help me." Someone from the boat threw a life preserver his way, but he was so tired he couldn't grab it. Ultimately, the man drowned. When he got to heaven, he asked God, "Why didn't you answer my call for help?" God said, "I sent you a log, a boat, and a life preserver. Did you expect me to come down and raise you out of the water myself?"

Ask for what you want, then let go, and let God, or the universe, or whatever you want to call it, deliver. Don't be a worrywart. Just keep moving with faith and trust in a universe that fulfills all your needs and desires.

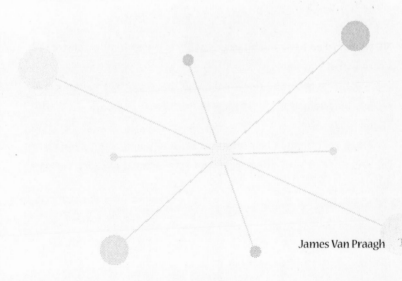

James Van Praagh

Oh, No! I Got What I Asked For!

So, you've asked for something. The universe is responding, but are you sure it's what you want?

What, are you crazy? I definitely want that cherry red Mustang convertible for graduation! Everyone will be jealous! I'll be the dude with all the chicks.

Okay, your thought becomes a reality. Your parents spring for a new car, and there in your driveway is your very own red Mustang convertible!

Now what?

You've become very popular, all right. Everyone wants a ride in your car. You didn't know you could be so popular, did you? You're out joyriding with every person who asks, Mr. Celebrity! I'm in now, you think. Girls are falling all over me. But is it you or the car they desire?

Would all these people hang out with you if you didn't have the car? Who can you trust? The truth starts to sink in. The thrill is gone. Now all you want is to be alone. You wish you could have your old car back and be yourself again.

Is there a message in all this? You bet. Be careful about what you ask for. You might just get it, and the unintended consequences that go with it.

Committing to Your Goal

Commitment! Now, *there's* a word that strikes terror in the hearts of any red-blooded teen. You know what I mean. You get an offer to go out with a friend on Friday night, but you don't really commit because you think something better might come along. So, you string your friend along until the last minute, just in case. Your friend decides you're a flake and blows you off. Then Friday night rolls around, and you're home alone. If you can't commit to one night out with a friend, what makes you think you can commit to something more complex, like passing your SATs or sinking shots for the basketball team?

Kim was a highly motivated gymnast since age ten. She was a member of a competitive team that constantly traveled to compete in regional tournaments. Kim's goal was to reach the national championship.

Kim and all of the other gymnasts were committed to their goal, and they practiced every moment possible. Over and over they would rehearse their tumbling, parallel bars, splits, and jumps. "I don't have time for a boyfriend," Kim said. "I have to concentrate all my energy on becoming a champion."

Not only was Kim committed to her present success, but she had a future goal to go on to a collegiate gymnastic team when she graduated from high school. Then, one day, Kim sprained her ankle when she lost her footing after a tumbling routine. Her foot in a cast, she spent the rest of the season on the sidelines. It was a blow to Kim, but she wasn't about to give up. "I'm no quitter," she said. "They're not going to push me out." So Kim showed up at every rehearsal and every team competition for the rest of the semester until her foot healed. "I have to be there if I want to go all the way to the national competition," she reasoned. Kim's team did win the regional championship, and she was there to receive the trophy with the rest of the girls. By the time her foot had healed, she was ready for the nationals. Her spirit of commitment certainly led her to her goal.

> A person without a plan always works
> for someone who has one.

How to Boost Your Commitment Level

To achieve your goal, you need commitment like Kim had. I know, it's scary looking down a long road to the end of a goal. So, commit one step at a time. In order to go from A to Z, you have to go through B, C, D, E, and the rest of the alphabet. If you take one step, you are that much closer to the end. Keep it simple and don't overwhelm yourself.

- Make sure your feelings are into your goal. Like Kim, you've got to love what you want.
- Follow your intuition. The universe will lead you to the next step.
- Take action one step at a time.
- Be grateful for every success along the way.
- Stay positive. When negative thoughts come up, tell yourself: Stop! Cancel that thought. Replace it with a positive thought. The universe hates a vacuum, which is what you leave when you delete something.
- Use love, not fear, in everything you do.
- Let go and have faith. Give the universe an opportunity to do its part by not trying to control the outcome. Sometimes, you may get better than what you expected.

Nothing is too good to be true.

List your goals for the next year, and one step toward each one you can take right now. Remember to prioritize. Don't go overboard and try to commit to a laundry list of goals. Pick the ones that are closest to your heart.

_____

_____

_____

_____

_____

SPIRIT SAYS . . .

You have to think about what you want.
Make sure your heart is in whatever you do.
Don't try to control the process.
Make your goal possible by going one step at a time.
Do what you say you want to do.
Trust the universe—it knows what you want.

Love + Forgiveness = Happiness

Give with a Grateful Heart

What Is Love?

Love is the energy that holds everyone and everything together. It's invisible like the air we breathe. We don't question air, so why would we doubt love? When we tap into the abundance of love, anything can be healed.

Love is the biggest reason we are here. In order to evolve as a spiritual being, you must learn to love. In every conversation I have had with spirit beings on the other side, the one thing I hear over and over again is that it doesn't matter how much money we have, or how many letters we amass after our names, or how much public status we gain. The only thing that matters is our capacity to love.

What will it take for you to be more loving? I'm not talking about the kind of love where you expect something in return, love that says things like "I love you if you love me," or "I'll love you when you give me a car." This is conditional love, and it's not real love. The love I'm talking about is unconditional. That's real love. When you love with no conditions, you open the door to everything in life.

Signpost #11: Love knows no limits.

Love Me for Me

Candace had been overweight since the age of ten. When she was in junior high, kids called her "Fat Ass" or "Pig Girl." Everyone always had a comment about her weight, even her teachers. "I had to stay after school because my teacher was mad that I couldn't fit into my desk," she recalled.

Candace tried to lose weight by going on diets, joining Weight Watchers, and taking pills. But whatever she lost always returned.

"I'm not allowed in phys ed because I'm too fat. Anyway, I don't want to be. I can't take all the jokes about how fat I am," she said.

Because she was not allowed in gym or any school sports, Candace was kept out of the very programs that might have helped her. On top of that, she could not even join a gym, either, because she was only fifteen.

Candace felt stuck, humiliated, vulnerable, and totally alone. She was depressed and sometimes wondered whether she would be better off dead. Her parents tried to support her efforts to lose weight, but they had weight issues of their own to deal with.

Candace wanted desperately to enter high school on a better foot. Her parents arranged to send her to a weight camp over the summer, and by the time fall came around she managed to lose forty pounds. "I just did what other normal kids are allowed to do. I was able to participate in sports and games and never even thought about eating. Losing weight wasn't an effort because I was moving around and enjoying myself."

Candace made friends with the other kids there, and they set up a support team, so that whenever she needed encouragement, Candace could call a counselor or another kid in the program. Someone was there to listen. Candace started to think that she might survive adolescence after all.

Candace's story is here because it is a story about love. Candace didn't like herself very much, never mind love herself. Negative thoughts ran through her mind constantly: How could anyone love me? They all make fun of me and laugh behind my back. I'm fat and no one will ever love me.

However, people did love Candace. Her parents, for instance—they wanted to help her help herself, so they sent her to camp. Her friends at camp loved her because they understood what it was like to be overweight and not accepted for the person inside. The counselors at camp loved her because they were sympathetic to her hopes and fears and wanted to see her succeed. Candace didn't know it, but she loved herself, too. She loved herself enough to do something about her predicament, and not just complain that she was destined to be overweight.

There was a lot of love at work in Candace's life, even if she didn't realize it herself.

Love can answer every need.

James Van Praagh 157

Let's take a closer look at love. Love is that indescribable thing we all want to feel. Think of all the times you have said or heard the words "I love you." We feel love, we romanticize it, and we talk about it. To me, love is the energy of the universe. It is the divine, unseen, unifying force that holds the molecules together. It is in us, it is around us, and it connects us. There is nothing that can control this force called love. It is the only real thing that exists, and you and I and everyone are made of it.

The Hardest Thing Is Letting Go

Candace had every reason to hold a grudge when everyone was hurling verbal sticks and stones in her direction. It's hard to get over that kind of humiliation. Fear, anger, bitterness, and resentment are very powerful feelings that keep away love, the very energy needed to help in such situations.

Without love, you can't do much. It's as if you lock your soul in solitary confinement. There's no getting out of the darkness until you let in some light.

Many times when we get hurt, we build an emotional wall around us. Rejection is hard to take. I don't need them, anyway, you tell yourself. You turn sullen and moody, or you withdraw behind a wall and become distant. "I don't care" becomes your mantra. Unfortunately, you do care.

"Love is the energy of the universe"

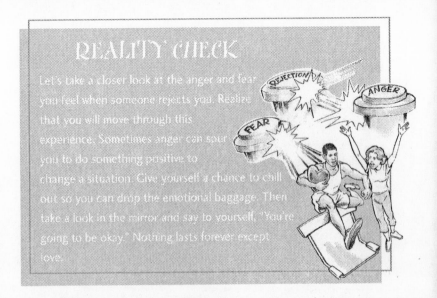

It takes a lot of courage to let go of a grudge. To have courage, you must believe in yourself. You must be willing to open your heart over and over despite life's hard knocks and unpredictable obstacles. No matter what, you have to let love into your heart so that you can heal the hurt.

Can You Forgive Me?

It was a hot summer evening in July. I was on the East Coast conducting a demonstration for a small group of people in someone's home. I am always amazed how Spirit finds the right individual, or in this case, individuals.

I was drawn to two young women sitting on a couch. Immediately, I turned to them and said, "Someone is here for you. She is a young woman about your age. Do you know the name Stacey?"

"Yes, I went to high school with her," one of the young women said.

"She died very suddenly. I am seeing glass and blood. She is pointing to her head. She was not prepared to die. Does this make sense to you?"

"Yes. In fact, I was thinking of Stacey just today."

"I get the feeling that she was very popular at school. She was a party girl."

Everyone in the room laughed.

"I see her in a car. I get the feeling that she was drinking or on drugs. Her head feels fuzzy. I see lots of glass. I think she was in a car accident. I'm sorry, but I think she went right through the windshield."

Both girls said at the same time, "Yes, that's right!"

"She tells me it happened after she left a party. She is saying, 'I was pretty messed up.' "

The two teens nod in agreement.

"She says she knows both of you. Is that right?"

I looked at both girls. "She is showing me a picture of the three of you in some sort of uniforms. Now she is showing me a football and the letter B."

"We were cheerleaders at school," said one of the girls. "The uniforms have B for Buchanan."

I was happy that they understood the information.

"She says she always wanted to be a mother. She is taking care of children where she is. She is like a social worker there."

The two young women smiled.

"This is strange. She is starting to cry. She is saying that she is very upset because of the way she treated you. She is telling me—forgive my French—that she was a bitch."

They both nodded their heads and said in unison, "You can say that again."

"She is telling me that she broke off her friendship with you two because she wanted to be with the more popular kids at school. She wanted to be in the in crowd. She says she was very jealous and always wanted to be the center of attention. Did you girls stop speaking to her?"

"Yeah, absolutely."

"She wants me to tell you she is very sorry. She was wrong. She is asking you to please forgive her. She says she was obsessed with being the most popular girl in school. She didn't care about your feelings. It was stupid of her."

The two girls began to get teary-eyed.

"'Will you please forgive me?' she says. It has been bothering her."

The two teens look at each other. "Yes, we forgive you, Stacey," they said together.

"She wants you to know she has felt your hurt, and it was awful."

I then explained to the girls, "Even when we leave our physical bodies, we still can feel the pain and anguish we have caused another person. We also have the opportunity to see the wrong we did and change. Stacey realized that she had many opportunities on earth to give love, but instead she chose jealousy and spite. With her new awareness, she wishes to be forgiven."

The session ended, and the two girls were happy that they had had a chance to connect with their friend Stacey and learn that the only way to be free is through forgiveness and love!

We cannot love until we forgive.

1. On a piece of paper, write about someone who has hurt you. Express all your feelings about this person and what he or she did to you. Write down any feeling that you still hold on to. When you're finished, fold the paper, and do the following meditation.

Now, close your eyes. Take three deep breaths. Visualize this person in a big bubble or balloon. You are safe because this person can no longer hurt or harm you. Now see the bubble floating up into the sky, dancing its way to heaven. As it soars away, you feel a sense of lightness, as all your hurt leaves with it. Finally, the bubble is out of sight, and you can open your eyes. Now take your folded piece of paper and flush it down the toilet. Know that your feelings of anger and resentment are going down with it.

2. Write down everything you have said or done to hurt another person. Express your feelings and your regret for having hurt this person. Fold your piece of paper, and do the following meditation.

Again, close your eyes. In your mind's eye, pick up an empty balloon and put the piece of paper inside. Blow up the balloon, tie off the end, and set it free. Watch as the balloon quickly soars away beyond the treetops. Now, picture the person you hurt receiving the balloon. She or he takes out the message inside and reads it. The person acknowledges your message and smiles. When you open your eyes, again take your piece of paper and flush it down the toilet. Know that your message has been received by the other person.

REALITY CHECK

When I tell people the way out of their pain is through forgiveness, I get a knee-jerk reaction of "not me!" Remember, forgiveness doesn't say bad behavior is okay. It really doesn't have to do with the other person at all. It has to do with you letting go of your resentment, anger, or fear. It takes a lot of compassion to say you forgive someone and mean it. But if you can do it, you can actually release the big chip on your shoulder. Your energy is freed up, and you can go on with your life.

Sometimes We Just Don't Know Why

I remember when seventeen-year-old Brad and his father came to see me. I couldn't help but notice all the rings Brad was wearing. Many parts of his face were pierced. At first, I wondered if the spirits would even tune in to the energy of this young man, because he seemed very closed off. But then I reminded myself that I had to let go of my judgment and ego and do what I was there to do. I recited my usual prayer and sat in silence waiting for contact with the other side.

A woman spirit appeared immediately. She was rather pretty and looked quite fragile. She had big blue eyes.

"There is a woman here. I feel this person is a mother figure. Does the name Nancy mean anything?"

At the mention of the name, Brad looked up at me in amazement. His father answered, "Yes. Nancy is my wife's name."

"Then she would be your mother?" I asked the boy.

James Van Praagh 155

Brad just nodded, not sure whether to trust me or not.

Still talking to the son, I said, "Your mother gives me the feeling that she was quite ill before she passed. I get the feeling that there were drugs or pills involved. Does this make sense?"

Brad did not answer my question. His dad replied softly, "Yes. That's right."

Then I got a visual that was quite heartbreaking.

"You found your mother in the bedroom, didn't you?"

The teen finally said something. "Yeah."

"Your mom is very sorry. She is asking you to forgive her. She didn't mean to cause you so much pain."

I paused for a moment. "I must tell you that I feel your mother was mentally not all there. I get the feeling that she was depressed a lot, and she couldn't help you."

"Uh-huh," he muttered. "My mother was always depressed, even when I was a kid."

"Your mother is apologizing for not being a very good mother to you. Was she in a mental institution?"

"Yes. In and out of them."

"She feels very off to me, like she is being pulled this way and that. She wants you to know that she loves you very much. She is so sorry for not being there for you and wants you to know she did love you when she was alive, in her own way." Then I said to Brad, "I am not sure your mother understood how to love."

Brad lifted his head. I could see tears forming in his eyes. This young man certainly had a lot of bottled-up emotions. His pain was great, and I could feel his anguish.

"I used to think it was my fault," he said. "I used to think she didn't want me around, that I was a pain in the neck to her. I didn't understand her. She was so moody. If I said the wrong thing, she would go off on a tangent and talk and talk until I couldn't stand it anymore."

He took a deep breath.

I spoke very softly. "I think your mother was her own worst enemy.

She was mentally ill, and she didn't know what she was doing. She is so sorry."

"Is she okay now?" Brad asked.

"Yes, she is okay. You know, there are sort of hospitals on the other side. Other spirits take care of all those people who were sick on earth. They help them to understand what happened to them. Your mother is with her family. She has work to do on herself, but she feels so much better."

"I'm glad. I'm so glad that she is not sick anymore."

At the end of the reading, I did a special prayer of healing for Brad and his dad.

As they got up to leave, the young man turned to me and smiled. I could feel his energy lifting.

"Thank you, Mr. Van Praagh. I feel much better myself. I feel I can get on with stuff now. You helped me a lot. Thanks."

Be Grateful for the Little Things

There is always something to be thankful for even when we think there isn't. That's what Brad realized. He thought his mother didn't love him, when all the time she did but just didn't know how to express herself because of her mental problems. It's amazing how much of Brad's energy changed when he forgave his mother and thanked me. It was as if a heavy suit of armor had dropped off him. It's hard to get around wearing a heavy suit of armor.

Finding the smallest of life's blessings can lighten your heart and open you up to new energy. You see, we do possess spiritual treasures inside, and we can live full, productive, and happy lives. There is a limitless supply of love always at our disposal. Turn your attention to love, and you will surely find it.

Like attracts like, I always say. Think of a boomerang. You throw it out into the sky, and it returns to you. When you send out love, love will return to you. It's as simple as that. You cannot receive what you do not give out.

People Are Different

When Dionne met Celia, they were like aliens from totally opposite planets. Celia was a petite, shy girl newly arrived from Hong Kong. Dionne was tall, popular, and fashionable. Dionne knew everyone, it seemed, while Celia knew no one. Celia was the Plain Jane type, and wasn't too hip as far as clothes and hairstyles were concerned. Dionne, on the other hand, had a great flair for what looked good and kept up with the latest styles in fashion and makeup. From all outward appearances, these two girls had nothing in common.

Celia had been a soccer player in China and tried out for the soccer team. She was a pretty good player, maybe even excellent. Dionne had very little interest in sports other than as a spectator, and then only at certain events.

"You've got to see this new girl play," said one of Dionne's friends.

"Play what?" Dionne replied.

"Soccer . . . she's great."

Dionne was not really interested in watching some girl play soccer. Now, if they had said some boy was playing . . .

Anyway, Dionne went to the soccer game with a crowd of kids and was amazed at the agility of this new midfielder. Dionne introduced herself to Celia at game's finish.

"Congratulations. It was an exciting game," Dionne said. Celia blushed.

Dionne decided to take Celia under her wing. She felt the girl needed some introduction into today's styles and trends.

Soon, the two girls went everywhere together. As Dionne showed Celia how to wear clothes, Celia taught Dionne how to eat with chopsticks. The girls found that exchanging cultural tastes and ideas was not only interesting but fun: they enjoyed teaching each other.

Even though the two girls came from completely different backgrounds, they found traits in each other that helped them grow as people. Dionne could have stayed with her group of familiar friends and never ventured out to learn something new, or she could have snubbed Celia altogether for being different. Instead, she embraced Celia's uniqueness, and their friendship flourished. Celia, meanwhile, could have just stuck to her soccer, something familiar, but instead she moved past her shyness and wanted to adapt to her new way of life and new country. Their differences brought out the best in them, and their friendship was a source of happiness for both.

Happiness is trying something new!

Can you find someone or something to be grateful for? Is it a friendship like Dionne and Celia's? List some of the things in your life that make you happy, even if they are seemingly small and insignificant, like watching a sunset.

_____

_____

_____

_____

REALITY CHECK

Let's take a look at gratitude. There is a law of the universe that goes something like this: If you don't like what you have, you're not going to get anything new. Have you ever noticed that people who have a lot get a lot more than people who have nothing? The rich get richer, the poor get poorer, that kind of thing. But I'm not talking about being wealthy in dollars and cents. I'm talking about being rich in love. You can have few material goods and still have a rich and rewarding life filled with friends, laughter, and fun. It's all in your attitude. Be grateful for the love you have to share—share it, and it will return to you ten times over.

SPIRIT SAYS...

Love is the energy that makes the world go around.
There is enough love in you to change what you don't like.
Forgiveness opens the way to your freedom.
Love attracts more love.
Gratitude is a good quality to have.

Take the High Road

Let Your Soul Inspire You

Build Your Own Support Team

Some of us are very old souls who have lived on earth many times before, and some of us may be new to earthly life. But no matter what, as you grow and experience new things, you will also face many problems, some of them perhaps for the first time. When problems do arise, each of us can benefit from support. There will be times when the support of others—parents, relatives, friends, teachers, and so forth—will be essential. No one travels through life alone.

Reach out to those who you feel will support you. Getting another person's perspective can be extremely helpful if you are in an emotionally charged, stressful situation. Even the most enlightened of souls can use support from someone who is emotionally uninvolved in the present predicament. It's a wise person who makes the most of everything and everyone available to help him- or herself.

Create a support team. List those people who you feel can help you without judgment or prejudice, and what they can offer you.

_____

_____

_____

_____

_____

Signpost #12: Support one another.

One Person Can Always Make a Difference

When I was a teen, my friend Connie was like another mother and mentor to me. She taught me to go beyond my fears and reach for my dreams, no matter what the odds. She bolstered my self-confidence and taught me to be true to myself. Her loving wisdom and heartfelt advice has helped me over many a rough spot.

Often I would feel as though I was nonexistent at home. Being the youngest of four children, I felt as if no one listened to me, nor did I feel that my parents believed me when I told them how much my brother and sisters would tease me. I remember one day when Mom went to the store and I was left alone with my brother. We fought over which television show to watch. Instead of my brother taking care of me, he locked me in the basement so he could watch his shows in peace. I screamed and kicked at the door, but no one heard me. I was stuck in the basement for hours; my brother freed me from captivity only shortly before Mom returned home. But I was afraid to tell on my brother because I knew he would do something to get back at me.

So I ran over to Connie's house and began to cry when she opened the door. She invited me in and gave me a glass of milk and some cookies. She listened to my story with great concern and sympathy. I felt better after spilling out my heart to her. She hugged me and said, "You're going to be all right." I looked into her eyes and knew that I would be. "You know, Jamie," she told me, "one day your brother and you will be the same size, and then you'll see him as a very good friend."

Connie was one of a kind, and she made a tremendous difference in my life. We can all use a Connie, and we can each be a Connie to someone else. Sometimes just listening can make all the difference in someone's life. You will get many chances to make a difference in the world. When you fill your backpack with kindness and caring, you have the capacity to change even the hardest heart and closed mind. Even with that, though, it takes courage to do the right thing.

When I was going to high school, I had a buddy, Lemar, whose father was a bus driver. Lemar's only ambition was to work for the city transit authority and become a bus driver like his dad. But his father refused to hear of such a thing. Instead, he wanted Lemar to go to college and become his own boss. Lemar was good at sports, so a college athletic scholarship was a possibility for him. But he was set on getting a city job. After all, it meant a steady gig with a retirement package.

Lemar's dad sent away for college admissions applications for his son. He was determined that Lemar "make something" of himself. Lemar didn't think he was smart enough for college, but he took his father's advice. He applied to college and also contacted the athletic departments of each school about scholarship opportunities. He was accepted at Ohio State University on a football scholarship.

The scholarship helped with tuition and books, but Lemar still had to work to meet his living expenses. So, while attending classes full-time and keeping a demanding regimen for football—a year-round commitment at a place like OSU—Lemar also worked a full-time job from four in the afternoon to midnight at a meat-packing plant. Even though it was hard work, Lemar realized that his dad was right—education *was* an important asset. Lemar went on to get his degree, and then went back to school to get an MBA. He now runs his own company, just as his dad had envisioned. Lemar supports his local YMCA and gives back to his community, just as his dad supported him. He counsels kids in low-income families to return to school and get an education.

The energy to make a difference is within each person. It doesn't take much to give someone encouragement. The wheel always comes full circle, and whatever you give out will always return to you.

Be a hero to somebody!

List some of the practical ways that you can give and share in your life.

_____

_____

_____

_____

_____

Get Your Motor Running

Without motivation, it's hard to get off your butt and make a difference. Here, then, are some ways to help you get started.

Tackle Small Jobs First

Be enthusiastic about routine chores. When you feel confident about doing a small task well, you will feel more self-assured. Remember that every-thing is energy, and each completed task builds a strong energy force in you. Bigger goals will not seem so tough.

Express Yourself

If you don't allow yourself to be a bystander in life, life will not seem so boring. Express your personality. You get to pick your personality for every lifetime, so express what your soul has chosen this time around. Communicate from your true self, not from your ego. Be adventurous and let your light shine!

Listen to Others

Spend more time listening to others. Don't try to control: allow others to choose for themselves even if you don't agree with their choices. Honoring the other person's decision tells them that it's okay to be themselves, and shows that you trust Spirit to make things right. You never know what is important for another person's spiritual growth.

Stay Focused on Your Good Qualities

It's too easy to fall into negative self-talk. Whenever you speak to yourself in less than loving terms, change your tune. Build a positive self-talk vocabulary, and you will attract positive things to you.

ATHLETIC
I'M ATTRACTIVE
I'M FORTUNATE
SMART
INTELLIGENT
LUCKY
TALENTED

Always Seek Something New

It's easy to stay in a rut and do the same old thing day after day.
It's comfortable—but monotonous at the same time. Try
something new. Study a new area of
interest. Join an organization and
volunteer your talents and abilities.
You will find that you can do a lot more
than you thought.

Have a Purpose

Start now to live a purposeful life. Spirit is constantly seeking expression
through your activities, thoughts, and achievements. Do what is important to you, and use goodwill in all that you do. You will help create a
better world for yourself, your family, and your friends.

Your Way or the High Way

I've talked a lot about ego in this book. Although it sometimes sounds
otherwise, let me say that ego is not a bad thing. Your ego is part of your
human personality. But it's like a puppy in training. If
you don't discipline a puppy, it will grow to be an un-
ruly and destructive dog. We all want to have a great
dog, or ego, that we can have fun with, but ultimately you (spirit) are the master, and ego is your
servant. It is not the other way around.

Last but not least, you must do the work if you
want to evolve as a spiritual being. This is not a hit-or-
miss process, nor is it a cheap trick. It requires respect,
humility, and discipline. The world outside is merely a
reflection of the world you have created inside. You create your own circumstances. There is no one like you.

James Van Praagh 155

Your uniqueness has been created from lifetimes of experiences. When you elevate your thoughts, you will open the treasure chest of gifts that is given only to you.

There are two ways to respond to any sticky situation. You can react, and allow the situation to determine what you do, which is what most people tend to do. Or you can take the higher ground and confront the problem and move on. Tough times can teach us to be compassionate and understanding. When we have compassion, we are acting from our soul's perspective.

Do ordinary things with extraordinary love.

Life Is What You Make of It

The world has grown smaller in the past decades. With computers, television, and telephones, we can instantly communicate around the globe to people of every culture. Never before have we been so closely linked to one another, and yet never before have people felt so alone. Far too many people lead unfulfilling lives. Many are like robots going through the motions. Others are slaves to their anger, hate, greed, and prejudice. On top of that, there always seems to be a war going on somewhere on earth.

In our country, we have been taught to respect the pursuit of money. We have been shown on TV that money and power pave the road to happiness, right? As we see each day, however, those with power and money can easily fall from their lofty perches. When you build castles on the sands of dishonesty, the negative energy comes back to destroy you. And this energy has a ripple effect, because it hurts others, too.

If all you want is to obtain money and material things in your life, you will find out that the road is filled with phonies and deadbeats.

You must remember that while your body is made up of bones, tissues, and organs, it is your soul that really gives your body life. Your purpose for living is not to be a slave to the lower aspect of your earthly personality. Always keep in mind that you are a being of light and love. A keen sense of your spiritual self promises a life of true happiness.

The following are some keys that will help you to reconnect to your soul.

Patience

Aggressive and impulsive behavior has been seen as cool, especially in sports, entertainment, and business. We want it all, right now! But when you are patient, you are cool. Literally. You don't let yourself get ruffled by every circumstance and situation. You pick and choose when to act or not act. You conserve your energy for the right moment. With this energy, you have power to make the right decision for you. I always advise people to meditate before taking action, because this allows spirit to guide you. Sometimes, the best course of action is to do nothing and let the situation mature and develop in its natural way. When you are impatient, you can make a situation worse. Being patient, on the other hand, helps to relieve the stress in your life. You make better decisions when you are not stressed out.

Balance

To live harmoniously, one must be in balance with both earthly and spiritual goals. When you spend all your energy on one thing, like sports for example, your schoolwork suffers. When you talk all day with your friends, you haven't had much time to listen to your own thoughts and feelings. Nature is always in a state of maintaining balance. A tree takes root where another has fallen. Create a balance among school, family, friends, and yourself, so that nothing and no one is deprived of your attention and love.

Sensitivity

Don't think of being sensitive as being a wimp. I am referring to sensitivity to your surroundings and other people. Too many of us get caught up in the thoughts of the masses, and it is hard to distinguish what we want from what we are told we want. Don't start criticizing or judging anyone without all the facts of a situation. Be open, yet question everything. Is this right for you? Are you hurting someone by your words or behavior? Are you helping? Can you do it differently?

Courage

A courageous person is not just one who risks his or her life for another. A person with courage is one with integrity. Integrity means honesty. Be honest; stay true to your feelings and your uniqueness when you make decisions and deal with others. When a problem arises, take a moment to listen to your heart, and do the best that you can do in that particular situation. Tomorrow is always another day.

Laughter

Being a spiritual being doesn't mean being a serious person. A sense of humor is a joy to everyone. Lighten up and the world laughs with you. There is a child in each of us wanting to laugh at life. How can we give the dense, complicated world such importance? It is our nature to express laughter and joy. Laughter actually transforms your body chemistry for the better. And anyway, you don't want to grow up and have all those frown lines on your forehead.

The Last Word . . . I Promise

Over the course of this book, I have given you twelve signposts to follow. These signposts are keys to playing the game of life and winning it. No matter what, always follow your heart. Never live someone else's life. You have to create your own road. Shine your light so that people can feel it around the world. You will find that your journey in this classroom called earth will have been worth it. You will return to your home in heaven with greater knowledge that you have left the earth a better place.

Write some of things you might like to accomplish in this lifetime. Don't limit your dreams!

_____

_____

_____

_____

_____

_____

SPIRIT SAYS . . .

Share your talents with the world.
Support a friend in need.
Elevate your thoughts with love.
Be patient with yourself and others.
Do the best that you can.
Laugh at life and it will laugh back!

Also available from Rider:

HEAVEN AND EARTH
Making the Psychic Connection

James Van Praagh

Millions of readers have been enthralled – and had their lives changed – by James Van Praagh's extraordinary ability as a psychic medium to communicate with the world beyond. In his global bestseller, *Talking to Heaven*, he took readers on a soul journey through time and revealed what happens in death, what the spirit world is like and how a soul is reborn.

Now, in this book, he combines inspiring accounts of his amazing communications with spirit beings with a practical programme for expanding our own innate psychic abilities and intuition. He explains that the spirits can serve us as teachers, companions, creative inspiration and even offer protection, once we learn:

- How to fully see, feel and hear
- How to strengthen one's aura to make contact
- How to recognize signals from spirit beings
- The role of angels
- Overcoming fear
- How to protect ourselves from negative or harmful forces

Heaven and earth are the two poles of our consciousness. This extraordinary work will show you how to connect the two within yourself and transform your understanding of life.

PROUD SPIRIT

Lessons, Insights & Healing from 'The Voice of the Spirit World'

Rosemary Altea

Known to millions as the 'Voice of the Spirit World' – through her first book, *The Eagle and the Rose* – Rosemary Altea is a British spiritual medium and healer. An international bestselling author, she draws clients from around the globe through her amazing ability to talk to the dead.

In this extraordinary book, she explores opportunities for spiritual growth in our everyday experiences. Using stories from her work and also from her personal life, she answers such questions as: Will our human personalities survive death intact? Are people in the spirit world affected by the actions of their loved ones on earth?

But this remarkable *tour de force* goes well beyond the subject of life after death, presenting awe-inspiring tales that shine a light on human conduct, such as the spine-tingling visit of children from the spirit world – or the story of an abused young boy who is kept safe by his guardian angel.

Hopeful, uplifting, strengthening, Rosemary Altea challenges us to know, value and be gentle with ourselves – to be *proud spirits*.

TEEN ANGEL

True Stories of Teenage Experiences of Angels

Glennyce S. Eckersley

Full or incredible true-life stories about angels and other psychic phenomena, this amazing book will make you hair stand on end – and open your heart.

Discover how angels have always existed, working for good against darkness. As well as guardian angels, there are angels of mystery, angels in nature, and angels who speak through that small inner voice guiding us. Angels can appear when we least expect them, and communicate through the power of music and strange coincidences.

Your very own angel may even be standing near you right now . . .

Buy Rider Books

Order further Rider titles from your local bookshop, or
have them delivered direct to your door by Bookpost

☐	**Heaven and Earth**		
	by James Van Praagh	1844130320	£5.99
☐	**Proud Spirit** by Rosemary Altea	071267117X	£7.99
☐	**Teen Angel** by Glennyce S. Eckersley	184413038X	£6.99
☐	**Spellbound** by Teresa Moorey	071261253X	£9.99
☐	**Lucky Stars** by Lori Reid	071265738X	£6.99
☐	**Dream Magic for Teenage Dreamers**		
	by Lori Reid	0712657487	£6.99

FREE POST AND PACKING
Overseas customers allow £2.00 per paperback

ORDER:

By phone: 01624 677237

By post: Random House Books
c/o Bookpost
PO Box 29
Douglas
Isle of Man, IM99 1BQ

By fax: 01624 670923

By email: bookshop@enterprise.net

Cheques (payable to Bookpost) and credit cards accepted

Prices and availability subject to change without notice.
Allow 28 days for delivery.
When placing your order, please mention if you do not wish to receive
any additional information.

www.randomhouse.co.uk